AMERICAN LAW

By Jang-Hean Jun

형설출판사
www.hyungseul.co.kr

머리말

인터넷시대에 살고 있는 오늘날 세계는 국경을 초월하며 경제 · 문화가 하나로 통일되어 가는 추세에 있으며, 그에 따른 법문화도 국제화 · 세계화가 이루어지고 있다.

이러한 국제화 · 세계화속에 오늘날 미국이 차지하는 경제, 정치, 법제도 등은 세계 각국에 중심에 있다고 하지 않을 수가 없다. 경제대국이면서도 다 민족으로 구성되어 있는 미국은 다양한 경제구조와 민주주의 국가체제하에서 법제도가 상당히 발전되어 각국에서 도입하고 연구해야 할 분야가 많은 현실에 있다.

그리고 미국 법은 다양한 사회적인 현실과 변화에 신속하고 능동적으로 대처할 수 있는 불문법주의를 취하고 있지만 상법 등은 일찍부터 성문법을 시행하고 있는데 그 내용의 정교함과 실체법에서 절차법으로 이어지는 법제도는 상당히 발전되어 있어 국제화가 진행되고 있는 오늘날, 미국 법에 대한 이해와 연구는 국제화 시대를 대비하는 초석이 될 수 있다.

이러한 미국 법에 대하여 본서는 주요 미국법과 판례에 대하여 영어원문을 수록 · 검토하여 미국 법체계와 법문화를 연구하고 나아가 한국법과의 비교 등에 주안점에 두어 기존의 도서와는 다른 학술서로서의 특징을 가지고 있다.

그리고 본서는 추상적이고 난해한 법리적인 관계에 대해서는 가능한 내용을 명료화 · 체계화함으로써 미국법과 판례 등에 대한 논점을 이해하고 해석이 가능하도록 하였으며 하루가 다르게 변화고 있는 국제화 시대에 미국 법에 대한 응용력과 논리적인 법학의 발전을 가져올 수 있도록 일관된 이론과 체계에 의하여 저술하였다.

막상 탈고를 하고 보니 수정하고 보완해야 할 부분이 많이 보인다. 앞으로 계속 보완하고 개선하여 좋은 책으로 만들고자 한다.

그동안 앞만 바라보며 살아온 세월이 많이 흘러간 것 같다. 지난 겨울 방학때는 모처럼 배낭과 텐트를 울러 메고 혼자 포카라에 있는 에베레스트 산을 가기 위해 네팔 행 비행기에 몸을 실었다. 옛날에 간적이 있어 고소적응기간 없이 5,000m이상의 신선 같은 아름다운 5개의 봉우리를 올라갔다가 귀국을 하였다. 앞으로 나에게 주어진 시간이 얼마인지 알 수 없으나 남은 시간동안 하늘의 도리에 순응하고 학문에 매진하여 나에게서 배운 학생들이 사회에서 요구하는 훌륭한 전문인으로 활동하고 한국법학의 발전에 조금이나마 도움이 되었으면 한다.

이 책을 저술함에 있어서 고마움을 표시할 분들이 너무나도 많다. 우선 본서는 복잡하고 난해한 미국판례와 성문법에 대하여 수많은 영문자료와 국내문헌 등을 참고자료로 하여 집필하였다. 이 책의 내용구성에 있어 참고가 된 수 많은 저술들의 저자분들께 감사한다. 그리고 저자의 은사이신 단국대학교 전 임정평 교수님, 권용우 교수님, 그리고 전 건국대학교 총장님이셨던 김용한 총장님, 이창석 교수님, 유병조 교수님, Pro. Neilson, Jessica과 주위의 모든 분께 이 자리를 빌어 깊은 감사를 드린다.

마지막으로 출판계의 어려운 여건 속에서도 본서의 출간을 쾌히 수락하여 주신 형설출판사 장지익 회장님과 심효섭 상무님, 최수환 과장님께도 감사의 뜻을 표한다.

2016년 6월
단국대학교 연구실에서
전 장 헌

차례

Chapter Ⅰ. Overview of Law

ChapterⅡ. CONTRACT

ChapterⅢ. TORT

Chapter Ⅳ. CRIMINAL PROCEDURE

Chapter Ⅴ. BUSINESS ASSOCIATIONS

Chapter Ⅵ. STRATEGIC MANAGEMENT

Chapter Ⅶ. PROPERTY

Chapter. I

Overview of Law

A. Introduction to law

B. Classifications of Law

C. Jurisprudence, or "What is Law?"

A. Introduction to law

We regularly encounter the law in our daily lives in driving cars, renting apartments, and on the job, anyone opening the newspaper or reading the news online in recent years would see articles discussing the legal debate over same-sex marriage, abortion, and legalization of marijuana and various high-profile trials.[1)]

This chapter provides the functions of law in society. Law performs many different functions in society. Law promotes social order and stability, but it can also be a force for change. Law seeks to establish justice, but law is no guarantee thereof. Law determines to a great extent how government operates, although law cannot ensure good government.

Fundamentally, law protects people and their property. To the social contract thinkers of the seventeenth and eighteenth centuries, this was primary purpose of law. Without law backed by

1 Matthew Lippman, Law and Society, SAGE Publications. Inc, 2015, p.2.

the coercive power of the state, people would have no choice but to protect themselves, their families, their land, and their possessions by force, at least ideally, protects the rights of the weak as well as the strong.[2)]

B. Classifications of Law[3)]

We have seen where law comes form. Now we need to classify the into different types. There are three main classifications that we use throughout the book : Substantive and Procedural Law, Public Law and Private Law, and Criminal and Civil Law.

---

2 John M. Scheb Ⅱ and Hemant Sharma, An Introduction to the Amercian Legal System, Wolters Kluwer–Law&Business, 2012, p.7; Austin Sarat and Patricial Ewick, The Handbook of Law and Society, Willey Blackwell, 2015, pp.3–8.

3 John M. Scheb Ⅱ and Hemant Sharma, An Introduction to the American Legal System, Wolters Kluwer–Law&Business, 2012, pp.12–13.

1. Substantive Law and Procedural Law

(1) Substantive Law

Substantive law defines rights and duties, such as crimes and punishments in the criminal law and civil rights and responsibilities in civil law. It is codified in legislated statutes, can be enacted through the initiative process and in common law systems it may be created or modified through precedent.

Defines the rights of the people. Substantive law defines the rights of people. Substantive law requires that a landlord who has singed a lease must deliver the store to her tenant. Usually Most of law concerns substantive law.

(2) Procedural Law

Procedural law comprises the rules by which a court hears and determines what happens in civil lawsuit, criminal or administrative proceedings. The rules are designed to ensure a fair and consistent application of due process or fundamental justice to all cases that come before a court. Substantive law, which refers to the actual claims and defenses whose validity is tested through the procedures of procedural law.

Procedural law established the processes for setting disputes. Procedural law requires that to get an injunction against Malfeasant, you must first notify her in writing of your claims and the time and place of the hearing on the injunction.

2. Public Law and Private Law

(1) Public Law

Sets the duties of governments to its citizens. Public law refers to the right and obligations of government as they deal with the nation's citizens. For example, when the Federal Trade Commission prohibits deceptive advertising, that is public law.

(2) Private Law

Regulates duties or right between individuals. Private law regulates the duties or rigth between individuals. Landlord−tenant law is private law.

3. Criminal Law, Civil Law, Administrative Law

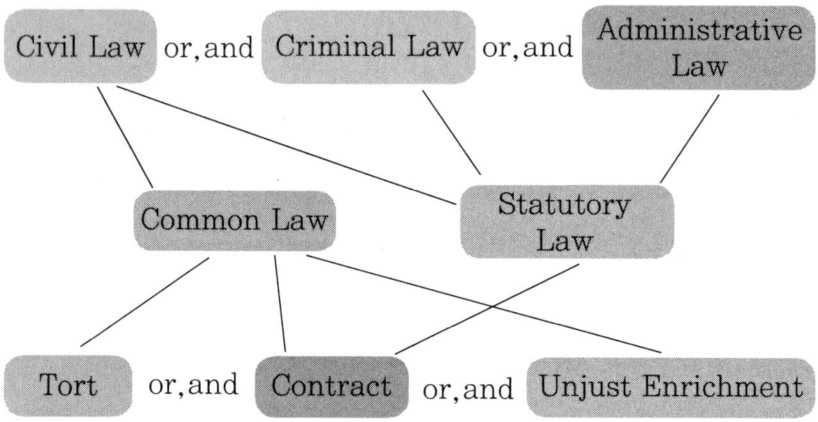

(1) Criminal Law

Criminal law is a branch of public law. A straight forward way of understanding criminal conduct is by viewing it as conduct which gives rise to legal proceedings through the prospect of state punishment. The criminal law is enforced by the state, infringements of the criminal law are punishable by the state.

Criminal liability and civil liability can, and frequently do, cross over. An act or an omission which simply means a failure to act may give rise to civil and or criminal liability. For example, if "A" hits "B" this could constitute the criminal offence of assault. It could also give rise to a civil action for trespass to the person(tort–civil law).

Therefore, if "A" hits "B" and is convicted of a criminal offence "A" may have to pay a fine. She might be sentenced to a term in prison or receive some other form of punishment for the offence. "A" may also have to pay damages under civil.[4)]

It is a crime to embezzle money from an bank, to steal a car, to sell cocaine. Criminal law concerns behavior so threatening that society outlaws it altogether.

Most criminal laws are statutes, passed by Congress or a state legislature. The government itself prosecutes the wrongdoer, regardless of what the bank president or car owner wants. A district attorney, paid by the government, brings the case to court. The injured party, for example the owner

4 John Hendy and Odette Hutchinson, Criminal Law, Routledge park squre, 2015, p.4.

of the stolen car, is not in charge of the case, although she may appear as a witness.

The government will seek to punish the defendant with a prison sentence, a fine, or both. If there is a fine, the money goes to the state, not to the injured party.

(2) Civil Law

The civil law regulates the rights and duties between parties. "갑" agrees in writing to Store lease "을" in her shopping mall. She now has a legal duty to make the space available. But she has violated her duty, but she has not committed a crime. The government will not prosecute the case.

It is you to file a civil lawsuit. Your case will be based on the common law of contract. "을" should win the suit, and get injunction and some money damages, But "갑" will not got to jail.

Some conduct involves both civil and criminal law. Suppose "갑" is so upset cover losing the court that she becomes drunk and causes a serious car accident. She has committed the crime of driving while intoxicated, and the state will prosecute. "갑" has also committed negligence, and the injured party will file a lawsuit against her, seeking money.

(3) Administrative Law

The basic unit of analysis of administrative law is the agency. Indeed, a good working definition of administrative law is "the law governing the forms, functions, and activities of government agencies."[5)]

The definition of an agency in the law is neither uniform nor precise. The most important, though by no means the only, federal statutory definition of an agency is contained in the Administrative Procedure Act, a statute that regulates many of the operations of federal administrative agencies.

Administrative law is the body of law that governs the activities of administrative agencies of government. Government agency action

5 "Agency" means each authority of the government of the United States, whether or not it is within or subject to review by another agency.

can include rule-making, adjudication, or the enforcement of a specific regulatory agenda. Administrative law is considered a branch of public law. As a body of law, administrative law deals with the decision-making of administrative units of government (for example, tribunals, boards or commissions) that are part of a national regulatory scheme in such areas as police law, international trade, manufacturing, the environment, taxation, broadcasting, immigration and transport. Administrative law expanded greatly during the twentieth century, as legislative bodies worldwide created more government agencies to regulate the social, economic and political spheres of human interaction.[6)]

(4) Conclusion

This definition raises some important distinctions that are worth addressing.

We make an analysis of the civil law, criminal

---

6 Gary Lawson, Federal Administrative Law, Thomson West, 2001, p. 1; From Wikipedia, the free encyclopedia

law, administrative law and Tort, Contract, and unjust enrichment through these one by one civil law.

1) Who the parties are plaintiff.? : as opposed to prosecutor. Tort, contract and unjust enrichment law provides for civil law rather than criminal law. Tort, Contract and unjust enrichment are disputes between private parties. In a tort. contract and unjust enrichment action the injured plaintiff bring suit against the defendant for damages. But Criminal action, the government will seek to punish the defendant with a prison sentence.

2) What the possible outcomes are liable?: as opposed to guilty. In criminal cases the defendant is found guilty or not guilty. But tort ,contract and unjust enrichment suit the defendant is Liable or not Liable

3) The applicable standard of proof: preponderance as opposed to beyond a reasonable doubt. Tort is the law of civil wrongs. In a criminal case the standard of proof is beyond a reasonable doubt. But In a civil case the standard approved with a few narrow exceptions is a preponderance of the evidence. The preponderance standard has been interpreted to mean that the finder of fact must be convinced that the plaintiff's assertions are "more likely than not" accurate.[7)]

4) The consequences for the defendant : civil damages as opposed to criminal penalties. The consequences for the defendant are different. If a criminal defendant is found guilty the penalties might include death, imprisonment and criminal fines. In a tort, contract and unjust enrichment suit, if the defendant is found liable the most common remedy is that the court will order the defendant to pay damages. Typically criminal fines are paid by the defendant to the government, but civil damages are paid by the defendant to the plaintiff.

---

7 Some courts have quantified this as more than 50 percent likely.

5) The procedural rules that apply : civil procedure as opposed to criminal procedure. The procedural rules are also different for civil as opposed to criminal. There are many differences between criminal procedure and civil procedure. The states are a lot different in criminal court than they are in civil court. In civil court we're talking about money or property. But in criminal court we're talking about jail time or probation. The rules and evidence are much different.

6) Tort, contract and unjust enrichment within civil law liability. There's also an important distinction between tort liability, contract liability and unjust enrichment liability. The definition of tort excludes breaches a contract, but contract law as binding promise. "A contract is a promise or set of promises for the breach of which the law gives a remedy, or the performance of which the law in some way recognizes as a duty." To an extent the Uniform Commercial Code does this :[8] "Contract

8 Uniform Commercial Code 1-201(1), Similarly in 1-201(2, 3).

means the total legal obligation which results from the parties" agreement as affected by this Act and any other applicable rules of law.[9] Tort law dictates the relationships between parties who have not had an opportunity to agree to a set of rules.

7) The English law of unjust enrichment is part of the English law of obligations, along with the law of contract, tort, and trusts. The law of unjust enrichment deals with circumstances in which one person is required make restitution of a benefit acquired at the expense of another in circumstances which are unjust.
English courts have recognised that there are four steps required to establish a claim in unjust enrichment. If the following elements are satisfied, a claimant has a prima facie
right to restitution :

- the defendant has been enriched;

9 Richard E. Speidel and Lan Ayres, Studies in Contract Law, Foundation Press, New York, 2003, p.1.

- this enrichment is at the claimant's expense;.
- this enrichment at the claimant's expense is unjust; and
- there is no applicable bar or defence.

The law of unjust enrichment is among the most unsettled areas of English law. Its existence as a separate body of law was only explicitly recognised in 1991 in 'Lipkin Gorman v Karpnale Ltd'. While the law has rapidly developed over the last two decades, controversy continues over the precise structure, scope and nature of the law of unjust enrichment.[10)]

C. Jurisprudence, or "What is Law?"

We have had a glimpse of Classifications of Law and a summary of the American Law. But what is law? That question is the basic of a field known as jurisprudence. How do we distinguish a moral rule form a legal rule? What is nature of law?

10 From Wikipedia, the free encyclopedia

1. Legal Positivism

This philosophy can be simply, Law is what the sovereign says it is. decisions stand, regardless of morality.

The sovereign is the recognized political power whom citizens obey, so in the United States, both state and federal governments are sovereign. A legal positivist holds that what ever the sovereign declares to be the law, whether it is right or wrong.

Therefore, Legal Positivism is law what the sovereign says.

2. Natural Law

An unjust law is no law at all and need not be obeyed. Laws must have a good moral basis. Letter from the Birmingham Jail, April 16, 1963 "There are two types of laws : just and unjust laws… A just law is a man-made code that squares with the moral law… An unjust law is a code that is out of harmony that is not rooted in eternal and natural law."[11)]

Therefore, Natural Law is that an unjust law is no law at all.

3. Legal Realism

Enforcement of the law is more important than the law itself. Enforces determine if the law is applied in a far and consistent way.

Legal realists take a very different tack. They claim it does not matter what is written as law. What counts is who enforces that law and by what process. All of us are biased by issues such as income, education, family background, race, religion, and many other factors. These personal characteristics, they say, determine which contracts will be enforced and which ignored, why some criminals receive harsh sentences while others get off lightly, and so on.

11 Natural Law Rev. Martin Luther King, Jr.

Judge Jones hears a multimillion dollar lawsuit involving an airplane crash. Was the airline negligence? The law is the same everywhere, but legal realists say that Jone's background will determine the outcome. If she spent 20 years representing insurance companies, she will tend to favor the airline. If her law practice consisted of helping the 'little guy' she will favor plaintiff.

Therefore, legal realism is that who enforces the law counts more than what is in writing.

▶ MEMO ◀

Chapter. II
CONTRACT

A. Overview Of Contract

B. Offer

C. Acceptance

D. Basic Principles

E. Common Law Remedies

A. Overview of Contract

1. What is a Contract?

- In this chapter, we examine the basic principles of contract. The right to contract is a core value in the united states, and the freedom of individuals, organization, and businesses to enter into contracts is basic to the free enterprise system.[12)]
- Stability in business arrangement, a promise for breach of which the law gives a remedy, or the performance of which the law in some way recognizes a duty.[13)]

12 John M. Scheb Ⅱ and Hemant Sharma, An Introduction to the Amercian Legal System, Wolters Kluwer–Law&Business, 2012, pp.236.

13 Richard E. Speidel and Lan Ayres, Contract Law, Foundation Press, New York, 2003, pp.12–35.

2. Elements of a Contract

(1) Agreement

- One party must make a valid offer, and the other party must accept it.
- One party must accept the other's offer.
- Example

A says to B : "If you promise to paint my building, I promise to pay you $ 1,000."

B says : "I agree."

Contract is formed when B agree.

(2) Bilateral Contract and Unilateral contract

What is a bilateral contract? There has to be bargaining that leads to an exchange between the parties. When most people think of contracts, bilateral agreements come to mind. In its most basic form, a bilateral contract is an agreement between at least two people or groups. Most business and personal contracts fall into this category.

Examples of bilateral contracts are present in everyday life. You're entering this type of agreement every time you make a purchase at your favorite store, order a meal at a restaurant, receive treatment from your doctor or even checkout a book at your library. In each circumstance, you've promised a certain action to another person or party in response to that person or party's action.

Unilateral contract is that unilateral contracts involve an action undertaken by one person or group alone. In contract law, unilateral contracts allow only one person to make a promise or agreement. You might see examples of unilateral contracts every day, too; one of the most common instances is a reward contract. Pretend you've lost your dog. You place an advertisement in the newspaper or online offering a $100 reward to the person who returns your missing pooch. By offering the reward, you're offering a unilateral contract. You promise to pay should anyone fulfill the obligation of returning your dog. You're the only person who has taken any action in this contract, as no one is specifically responsible or obligated to finding your dog passed on this interaction.

Bilateral and Unilateral contracts are difference. At first glance, the most obvious difference between bilateral and unilateral contracts is the number of people or parties promising an action. Bilateral contracts need at least two, while unilateral contracts only obligate action on one part. The other differences might be a bit more subtle. Look at what's being offered. In unilateral contracts, one offering the deal promises to pay when a certain act or task is complete, but bilateral contracts allow for an upfront exchange. Both unilateral and bilateral contracts are enforceable in court. For example, a unilateral contract is enforceable when someone chooses to begin fulfilling the act demanded by the promisor. A bilateral contract is enforceable from the get-go; both parties are bound the promise.[14)]

---

14 www.rocketlawyer.com/article/whats-the-difference-between-

(3) Past(moral) consideration is no consideration

Moral obligation is generally unenforceable for lack of consideration[15]. Moral consideration is no consideration.

The law has as one of its main functions to guide behavior, by telling people what to do or not to do in the from of prohibiting and prescribing acts. However, most of morality is not concerned with guidelines for behaviors. Morality primarily sets standards through which we can evaluate behavior as "good.", "not so good." or simply "bad." Good and bad come in degrees, better or worse. From the legal point of view, a particular act is either permitted or not, without such grey areas.

Moreover, moral norms and standards are normally considered to be important for the well-

---

bilateral-and-unilateral-contracts.rl;Rocket Lawyerhttps; 부산지법 2009가합17403에서 "동시이행의 관계에 있는 쌍무계약에 있어서 상대방의 채무불이행을 이유로 계약을 해제하려는 자는 동시이행관계에 있는 자기 채무의 이행을 제공하여야 하는데, 매수인인 원고가 매매잔대금이 예치되어 있는 예금통장의 사본을 피고에게 제시한 것만으로는 이행의 준비태세를 갖춘 것에 불과하지 적법한 이행 제공이라고 볼 수 없다는 이유로 매매계약 해제를 원인으로 한 원고의 매매대금반환청구를 기각하였다". 쌍무계약에서는 동시이행의 관계에 있으며 상대방이 채무를 이행할 때까지 이행연체에 따른 손해배상의무가 발생하지 않는다.

15 Richard E. Speidel and Lan Ayres, op. cit, pp.109-112.

functioning of society, while this is not necessarily the case for all legal rules.[16)]

(4) Legality

The contract must be for a lawful purpose

3. Case[17)]

(1) FACTS

- The defendant had assaulted his wife, who took refuge in plaintiff's house. The next day the defendant gained access to the house and began another assault upon his wife. The defendant's wife knocked him down with an axe, and was on the point of cutting his head while he was laying on the floor, and the plaintiff intervened, caught the axe as it was descending, and the blow intended for defendant fell upon her hand which

16 Jaap Hage · Bram Akkermans, Introduction to Law, Springer International Publishing Switzerlan, 2014, p.3.

17 JSupreme Court of North Carolina, 1945. 225 N.C. 690, 36 S.E. 2d 227.

was wounded badly, but saving defendant's life.

- Subsequently, the defendant orally promised to pay the plaintiff her damages; but after paying a small sum, failed to pay anything more.

(2) ISSUES

Was there a consideration recognized by our law as sufficient to support the promise?

(3) HOLDING : No

(4) RATIONALE

A Voluntarily performed humanitarian act of this kind is not a legally recognized consideration for the later promise.

B. Offer[18)]

1. When an offer is

- clear
- definite
- explicit
- write or oral
- measurable

it constitutes an offer, acceptance of which completes the contract.

2. Communication

(1) The offeror may withdraw his offer until communication.

(2) Offers are destroyed by unreasonable lapse of time.

- rejection.
- counteroffer.

18 Richard E. Speidel and Lan Ayres, Contract Law, Foundation Press, New York, 2003, pp.245–260.

3. Case[19)]

(1) FACTS

- The defendant publishes an advertisement in a newspaper as follows : "Saturday 9 A.M. New Fur Coats Worth to $ 100.00 First Serve $ 1 Each."
- The plaintiff second visited the defendant's store and demanded the coat. The defendant refused to sell the coat by stating that the offer was intended for First woman only by a "house rule."
- The plaintiff sued the defendant for the damage for breach of contract.

(2) ISSUES

Did the ads constitute an offer, and if so, did the conduct constitute an acceptance?

(3) HOLDING

The ad did not constitute an offer.

19 Supreme Court of Minnesota 1957.

(4) RATIONALE

- When an offer is clear, definite, and explicit, it constitutes an offer.
- The meaning of the fur coats mentioned in the ad was uncertain, and therefore, it does not constitute an offer.

4. Cases[20)]

(1) FACTS

- plaintiff operated an extensive milling business. The crank shaft which operates the broke and, as a result, all work stopped.
- plaintiff was required to send the shaft.
- The delivery of the shaft was delayed and as a result the mill was shut down for several days. The mill thus lost profits it would otherwise have received, and plaintiff filled suit to recover these damages.

20 Court of Exchequer, 1854. 9 Exch. 341, 156 Eng. Rep. 145 ; Supreme Court 1993. 10. 22, 93

(2) ISSUES

Should the defendant be liable for the plaintiff's loss of profits due to the defendant's breach when the plaintiff has not communicated his special needs to the defendant?

(3) HOLDING : No

(4) RATIONALE

- These special circumstances were never communicated by the plaintiffs to the defendants.
- These special circumstances were wholly unknown to the party breaking the contract.

C. Acceptance[21)]

1. One party must accept the other's offer. The power to create a contract by acceptance of an offer.

---

21 Richard E. Speidel and Lan Ayres, Contract Law, Foundation Press, New York, 2003, pp.284-323.

2. Definite

(1) The agreement shall become binding upon written acceptance or commencing performance of the work.[22]

(2) When an acceptance is

- definite
- explicit
- write or oral
- reasonable

3. Communication of acceptance

- There is no contract until acceptance of an offer is communicated to the offeror.
- If an offer demands acceptance in a term validity, the offeree must follow those requirements(Civil Law §528 ①).
- When the contract does not specify a time for acceptance, a reasonable time is allowed.

22 Korea civil law §532.

4. Cases[23)]

(1) FACTS

- Defendants signed an instrument for the purpose of obtaining the service of plaintiff in re–roofing their house.
- The instrument was signed by plaintiff's friend who was without authority to accept for the plaintiff.
- The plaintiff prepared this work(engaging workmen and two truck, and so on).
- Upon their arrival at defendant's residence, defendants notified the work had been contracted to other parties.

(2) ISSUES

- Is plaintiff's commencing the work(preparing for the work, engaging working....) the power of acceptance?
- Who is an Agent?

23 Court of Appeal of Louisiana 1998 ; Supreme Court 1996. 1. 26. 95다26919 korea.

(3) HOLDING : Yes

(4) RATIONALE

- It was the intention of plaintiff to accept by commencing the work[24], which was one of the way provided for in the instrument for acceptance. It was possible to create acceptance of an offer by the end of a "reasonable time". Defendant knew this was to be processed through plaintiff's office. The Plainfiff appeared to start work on the Defendant's roof only to find another team at work.
- Restatement explains key terms, ㉠ Agency : a fiduciary relationship resulting from consent of one person to another that the other shall act on his/her behalf. ㉡ Principal : one whom action is taken for. ㉢Agent : one who is to act. Consent, control and a fiduciary relationship are required. Elements not

24 korea civil law §532.

required for an agency relationship include : A written agreement (unless the business of the agent requires a written contract). formal agreement (acting like agent and principal is enough to establish agency). Consideration (an agent does not have to be paid).

D. Basic Principles[25)]

1. When does breach occur?

- If a promisor is found to be under an absolute duty to perform, and her duty has not been discharged by performance or otherwise, her failure to perform at the time and place provided in the contract constitutes a breach thereof.
- BREACH=failure to perform that which under absolute duty to perform, without justification

25 Richard E. Speidel and Lan Ayres, Contract Law, Foundation Press, New York, 2003, pp.191–210.

or excuse.

2. Contract Remedies protect three interests

(1) Expectation interest

- Remedies that protect this interest seek to put a promisee in the position she would have been in if the breaching promisor had performed.
- Using this approach gives the injured promisee the benefit of her (2) bargain.

(2) Reliance interest

- Contract remedies sometimes seek to put the promisee in the position she would have been in if she had not entered into the contract.
- Contract law protects the promisee's reliance interest by reimbursing the promisee for loss caused by relying on the contract.

(3) Restitution interest

- Contract law sometimes tries to protect the

promisee's restitution interest by requiring the breaching promisor to return to the promisee any benefit received by the breaching promisor.

- The injured party may be unable to show and expectation interest or reliance. But perhaps she has conferred a benefit on the other party. Here, the objective is to restore to the injured party the benefit she has provided.
- Example, "갑" signed a contract to sell 10,000m2 of land to "을". "을" was to take possession immediately, but would not receive the deed until he finished paying for the property, in 10years. "을" did move on to the land and did receive $100,000 from the government for a year's worth of inactivity.

The only part of the bargain "을" did not keep was his promise to pay. "갑" sued. "을" had breached the deal. But what remedy? "갑" still owned the land, so she did not need it reconveyed. "을" had no money to pay for the farm, so the "갑" would never get their expectation interest. And "갑" had expended almost no money based on the deal, she had no reliance interest. What she had done, though, was to confer a benfit on "을". "갑" had enabled to obtain $100,000 in government money. "갑" wanted a return of the benefit "갑" had conferred on "을". a remedy called restitution .The restitution interest is designed to return to the injured party a benefit that she has conferred on the other party, which it would be unjust to leave with that person.

3. Specific performance

Contract law typically provides for substitutional relief in the form of an award for money damages, instead of specific relief in the form of a court order that requires the breaching party to perform.[26)]

26 Terry Halbert and Elaine ingulli, and Law & Ethics in the Business Environment, Cengage Learning, 2015, pp.310-322.

(1) Rest 2nd §359(1)

Specific performance or an injunction will not be ordered if damages would be adequate to protect the expectation interest of the injured party.

(2) UCC §2-716

Specific performance may be decreed where the goods are unique or in other proper circumstances.

E. Common Law Remedies

1. Expectation Interest[27)]

The injured party has a right to damages based on his expectation interest as measured by the loss in the value to him of the other party' s performance caused by its failure or deficiency, plus any other loss, including incidental or

27 Richard E. Speidel and Lan Ayres, Contract Law, Foundation Press, New York, 2003, pp. 889-921.

consequential loss, caused by the breach, less.[28)]

This is the most common remedy that the law provides for a party injured by breach of contract. The expectation interest is designed to put the injured party in the position she would have been in had both sides fully performed their obligation. A court tries to give the injured party the money she would have made from the contract. If accurately computed, this should take into account all the gains she reasonably expected and all the expenses and losses she would have incurred. The injured party should not end up better off than she would have been under the agreement, not should she suffer serious loss.

Example "A" was a former director of the 'Central Intelligence Agency'. He wanted to write a book about his 10years of experiences in 'Iraq War'. He paid "B" $100,000 for help in written an early draft, published and promised. But "B" was hopelessly late and missed his publication date. "C" published several years late, and the book

28 Rest 2nd §347

flopped, earning no signification revenue. Because the book was so late. So, “A” sued “B” for his lost expectation interest.

(1) Compensatory Damages

Compensatory damages are the most common monetary awards for the expectation interest. Courts also refer to those as ‘direct damages’ Compensatory damages are those that flow directly from contract. In other words, these are damages that inevitably result from the breach.

Suppose “갑” hires “을” to star in its new movie.

In side Straight. “갑” promises $3million, providing she shows up May 1 and works until the film is finished. But in late June, “병” offers “을” $5million to star in its new feature, and on July 1 “을” inform “갑” that she will not appear. “을” has breached her contract, and “갑” should recover compensatory damages.

When are the damages that flow directly from the contract? “갑” obviously has to replace “을”. If “갑” hires “정” as its star and pays her a fee of

$4million, "갑" is entitled to the difference between what it expected to pay $3million and what the breach forced it to pay $4million, or $1million in compensatory damages.

(2) Consequential damages

The injured party can also recover other losses caused by the breach so long as those losses were reasonably foreseeable to the breaching party at the time of formation.

Consequential damages are those resulting from the unique circumstance of this injured party.[29] The rule from Hadley v. Baxendale has been unchanged ever since, the injured party may recover consequential damages only if the breaching party should have foreseen them.

Example, "A" had sold the film's soundtrack rights to "B" for $2million. "B" believed it would make a profit only if "C" appeared in the film, so it demanded the right to discharge the agreement

29 This rule concerning this remedy comes from a famous 1854 case, Hadley v. Baxendale.,

if "C" dropped out. When "C" quit, "B", terminated the contract. Now, when "A" sues "C", it will also seek $2million in consequential damages for the lost music revenue.[30)]

(3) Incidental damages

- Incidental damages include reasonable costs that the injured party incurs to try to avoid loss after the breach.
- Incidental damages are the relatively minor costs that the injured party suffers when responding to the breach. When "A" singer, breaches the recording contract, the producers may have to leave the set and fly back to seoul to hire an new actress. The travel cost is an incidental damage. In another setting, suppose "A" manufacturer, has produced 2,000 pairs of running shoes for "B", a retail chain, but "B" breaches the agreement and refuses to accept the goods."A" will have to store the

9Ex. 341. 156 Eng. Rep. 145 Court of Exchequer. 1854.

30 Jeffrey F. Beatty and Susan S. Samuelson, Business Law and the Legal Environment, Thomson Southwestern, 2004, pp.395–396.

shoes and advertises for alternate buyer. The storage and advertising costs are incidental expenses, and "A" will recover them.

- The injured party may recover, as incidental damages, the reasonable costs of mitigation.

2. Reliance Interest

- A court can award damages based on the injured party's reliance interest, in lieu of awarding damages based on the injured party's expectation interest.
- The injured party's reliance damages equal. The expenditures the injured party made to prepare to perform or to perform, less any loss that the injured party would have suffered if the breaching party had performed.

3. Specific Performance

Specific performance is an equitable remedy by which a party to a contract is ordered to perform according to its terms. The injured party may receive specific performance of a contract only where money damages for breach would be "inadequate"[31) For example, if "A" owned building. She sold it to her sister in law, "B". "B" granted an option to buy additional property at $100 million. "B" could exercise her option anytime during A's lifetime or within six months of A's death. When A died, B informed the estate's executor that she was exercising her option. But other relatives wanted the property and the executor refused to sell. B sued and asked for specific performance. She did not want an award of damage, she wanted the estate itself. The remedy of specific forces the two parties to perform their contract.

A court will award specific performance, ordering

31 Richard E. Speidel and Lan Ayres, Contract Law, Foundation Press, New York, 2003, pp.968-992.

the parties to perform the contract, only in cases involving the sale of estate or some other asset that is unique. Courts use this equitable remedy when money damages would be inadequate to compensate the injured party. If the subject is unique and irreplaceable, money damages will not put the injured party in the same position she would have been in had the agreement been kept. So a court will order the seller to convey the rare object and the buyer to pay for it.[32)]

32 Jeffrey F. Beatty and Susan S. Samuelson, Business Law and the Legal Environment, Thomson Southwestern, 2004, p404.

Chapter. Ⅲ
TORT

A. Introduction to Tort Liability

B. Negligence Principle

C. The Duty of Physical Injuries

D. The Duty of Non-Physical Injuries(Emotional Harm)

E. Causation

F. Damages

A. Introduction to Tort Liability[33]

1. Meaning

The fundamental issue addressed by a system of tort liability for unintended injury is when losses should be shifted from an injury victim to an injurer or some other source of compensation.

The rules of tort law can, to some extent, be explained by the fact that tort law fulfills several functions These functions include the realization of compensatory justice, the realization of a distribution of damage over society that is both fair and efficient, the granting of compensation to people for damages caused by someone else, the prevention of damages.[34]

The courts have developed a complex network of liability rules for determining the allocation of losses in cases of unintended harm. These rules, located in an intermediate zone between no-

33 Marc A. Franklin and Robert L. Rabin, Tort Law and Alternatives –cases and materials–, Foundation Press, New York, 2001, pp.1–28.

34 Jaap Hage · Bram Akkermans, op. cit, p.103.

liability and universal compensation, reflect not only the influence of those polar positions, but perhaps even more importantly, a tension between two court-fashioned liability principles strict liability[35)] and negligence that will be a pervasive concern of ours in this court.

There is three main types of tort liability. Intentional Tort is that Focus on intent of Tortfeasor&Prima facie[36)] showing of tort.

Negligence tort is that focus on the tortfeasor's duty of care and reasonable person standard. Strict liability tort is that the facts speak for themselves(no need to show intent or tortfeasor's duty of care). In other words, Intentional torts, Negligence and Strict liability. Intentional torts and Negligence are

35 Terry Halbert and Elaine ingulli, and Law & Ethics in the Business Environment, Cengage Learning, 2015, p. 307; In 1963, the California Supreme Court adopted what is now called 'strict liability'. This new legal theory made it easier for injured persons to sue and harder for manufactures who sold defective products to defend themselves. Strict liability recognizes that there are times when loses must be allocated between two innocent parties: the consumer who was hurt while using a product properly and the company that was not negligent(careless) in creating it. It places the responsibility on the company for reasons articulated here by noted legal scholar William Prosser in "The Fall of the Citadel".

36 Prima Facie Evidence is same with Prima Facie showing that is definite evidence.

based on wrongdoing or fault by the defendant.

Strict liability is something else altogether. It's made up a few exceptional situations where the law assigns liability to the defendant, even where the harm was caused by accident unlike intentional torts and even where the defendant with careful unlike negligence.

For example, the defendant store owner sells a defective remanufactured blender which malfunctions injuring the plaintiff. The defendant store owner may be liable, even though he wasn't responsible for causing the manufacturing defect and even thought he could not reasonable be expected to have discovered the defect before the sale. Because the defective blender looked just like all the other blenders. It received from the manufacturer the idea behind strict liability. In strict liability, the law assigns the costs of the consequences of the defendants's activity to the defendant.

2. Tort Means "Wrong"

A tort is a violation of a duty imposed by civil law.

(1) Defamation[37] : making a false or truth statement about someone – written or verbal.

(2) Negligence : performing wrong surgery.

(3) Interference with contract : stealing a client away from a competitor.

(4) Fraud : offering to sell something that doesn't exist.

3. Tort vs. Criminal or Contract law

Tort law must be distinguished from both contract law and criminal law. Unlike contract

37 Korea criminal law: Article 307.

law, Tort law deals with situations where there is no preexisting contractual relationship. If such a contractual relationship does exist, compensation of damage is usually dealt with by the law of contract.

Moreover, unlike criminal law, tort law does not aim at punishing wrongful behavior, but seeks for ways to compensation the damages that is often caused by wrongful acts. So tort law differs from criminal law in that it does not focus on punishment but on the compensation of damages, and it differs from contract law in that it does not deal with the damages that results from the nonperformance of contract.[38)]

(1) Criminal Law

Criminal Law behavior classified as dangerous to society ; prosecuted by the government, whether victim wants to prosecute or not ; money award goes to the government.

---

38 Jaap Hage · Bram Akkermans, op. cit, pp.102.

(2) Contract Law

Contract Law based on breach of an agreement between the two parties ; victim prosecutes and receives compensation or restitution.

(3) Tort Law

Tort Law based on an obligation imposed by the law with no agreement needed between parties ; victim prosecutes and receives compensation or restitution.

4. Unintended injuries Result in liability

(1) The Unintentional Tort

Courts have developed a complex network of liability rules for determining the allocation of losses in cases of unintended harm	

To win a negligence case, the plaintiff must prove that the defendant failed in five areas

1) Duty of due care

There must be a duty owed to the plaintiff.

2) Breach

The defendant breached her duty

3) Factual cause

The injury must have been caused by the defendant's actions

4) Foreseeable harm

It must have been foreseeable that the action would cause this kind of harm.

5) Injury

The plaintiff must have been hurt

(2) In Hammontreee v. Jenner

The Court recognized that, The liability of a driver, who suddenly stricken by an illness rendering him unconscious, for injury resulting from an accident occurring during that time must rely on general principles of negligence(Not on the doctrine of strict liability). therefore, Hammontree(Plaintiff) injury, resulting from the seizure which rendered him unconscious, depends on principles of negligence. Doctrine of strict liability does not apply in this case.

(3) Assumption of the Risk

A Person who voluntarily enters a situation that has an obvious danger cannot complain if she is injured. This rule applies to situation where the danger is well-known and the participant chooses to be present.[39]

39 http://news.sbs.co.kr/news/endPage.do?news_id=N1000902116:서울중앙지법 민사합의26부는 아프가니스탄에서 살해된 샘물교회 신도 A 씨의 유족이 국가를 상대로 낸 손해배상 청구 소송에서 원고 패소 판결했다. 재판부는 정부가 다양한 언론매체 등을 통해 아프간의 정세가 불안정하고 탈레반의 테러 가능성을 알렸으며, 아프간 여행을 원하는 사람들에게 이 내용을 일일이 알리기는 현실적으로 어렵다고 밝혔다. A 씨의 부모는 외교통상부가 아프간 여행객에게 직접 위험을 알리거나 출국 자제 요청을 하지 않았다며 3억 5천만 원의 손해배상 청구 소송을 냈었다. 그러나 법원은 'Assumption of the Risk'의 논리에 따라 자진하여 위험지역임을 알면서 진입하여 사고가 발생한 경우 손해배상의무가 없다는 판결을 결정했다.

5. Intentional Torts

(1) Meaning

An intentional tort is a category of torts that describes a civil wrong resulting from an intentional act on the part of the tortfeasor (alleged wrongdoer). The term negligence, on the other hand, pertains to a tort that simply results from the failure of the tortfeasor to take sufficient care in fulfilling a duty owed, while strict liability torts refers to situations where a party is liable for injuries no matter what precautions were taken.[40] Intentionally throwing an object, but not meaning to hit anyone is a tort if it causes injury to someone. Includes business torts, a category of torts perpetuated almost exclusively by business entities.

(2) Defamation

1) Defamation is irresponsible speech to harm

40 https://en.wikipedia.org/wiki/Intentional_tort

another's reputation.

- Written defamation is libel.
- Verbal defamation is slander.

2) There are four facts to prove to win a defamation suit.

- The defamatory statement was actually made.
- The statement is false.
- The statement was communicated to someone other than the plaintiff.
- In slander cases, the plaintiff must show some injury that resulted from the defamation.

3) Slander per se : some statements are so harsh and potentially damaging that the plaintiff is assumed to be damaged and does not have to prove injury.

- Accusations of committing a serious crime.
- Claims of having a sexually transmitted disease or of being an unchaste woman(gender bias in the law).
- Alleged professional incompetence.

4) Opinion : to be defamation, the statement must be provable and not simply someone's opinion.

- Vague terms in the statement usually indicate it is an opinion, not a provable fact.
- Extreme exaggerations are usually not taken as fact.

5) Public Personalities

- Includes : public officials(police and politicians) and public figures(movie stars and other celebrities).
- Public personalities : Public personalities have a harder time winning a defamation case because they have to prove that the defendant acted with actual malice.

6) Privilege

- Defendants receive extra protection in special cases.
- In courtrooms and legislatures, speakers have absolute privilege. They may speak freely, as long as it is true.

- When information is legitimately needed, the speaker giving it has qualified privilege. This may happen when someone reports a suspected criminal act.

(3) False Imprisonment

False imprisonment is the restraint of someone against their will and without reasonable cause. An employer who doesn't let a sick employee go home might be guilty of false imprisonment. If the police detain a person with no reason to suspect him of any crime, it could be false imprisonment.

In general, shopkeeper may detain a person suspected of shoplifting if there is a reasonable basis for the charge and the detention is done reasonably(in private and for a reasonable time).

(4) Intentional Infliction of Emotional Distress

Injury was only emotional instead of physical. Today, most courts allow a plaintiff to recover from a defendant who intentionally causes emotional injury. Behavior causing injury must be extreme and outrageous. Must have caused serious emotional harm. Some courts allow recovery for emotional injury caused by negligent behavior.

(5) Battery and Assault

1) Battery is a touching of another person in a way that is unwanted or offensive.

- ■ The touch does not have to hurt the victim.
- ■ sexual touching that is offensive, but not painful, is battery.
- ■ An intentional action that does hurt someone may be battery even if the injury is unintentional.

2) Assault is an action that causes the victim to fear an imminent battery.

- ■ Assault can occur without the battery ever happening.
- ■ Pulling a gun on someone.

(6) Trespass, Conversion, and Fraud

1) Trespass is intentionally entering land that belongs to someone else or remaining after being asked to leave.

- Keeping an object, such as a vehicle, on someone else's land and refusing to move it is also trespassing.
- You may be trespassing if you enter someone's property mistakenly believing it is public property.

2) Conversion is taking or using someone's property without consent(civil law version of theft).

3) Fraud is injuring another person by deliberate deception.

6. Liable of the employer by employee's act

(1) Under the doctrine of Respondent superior, employers are vicariously liable for torts committed

by employees acting within the scope of their employment.

(2) Three criteria useful in the determination are as following.

- The employee's conduct must be of the general kind the employee is hired to perform.
- The employee's conduct must occur substantially within the hours and ordinary spatial boundaries of the employment.
- The employee's conduct must be motivated, at least in part, by the purpose of serving the employer's interest.

B. Negligence Principle[41)]

1. The Standard of Care

What is Negligence?

Negligence is the doing of something which a reasonably prudent person would not do, or the failure to do something which a reasonably prudent person would do, under circumstances similar to those shown by the evidence. It is the failure to use ordinary or reasonable care.

Most tort lawsuit are based on negligence. Negligence behavior is common. We all make mistakes, then we are insured against our mistakes.[42)]

41 Marc A. Franklin and Robert L. Rabin, Tort Law and Alternatives −cases and materials−, Foundation Press, New York, 2001, pp.85−108.

42 Multistate Legal Students, INC, PMBR part a−multistate specialist−, Multistate Legal Students, INC, 2004, p.16.

2. Historical Development of Fault Liability

- Fact : Brown's dog was fighting against Kendall's dog. Kendall, while trying to separate the dogs with a long stick, accidentally hit Brown's eye. This case proceeds on the assumption that the damage sustained by Brown(plaintiff) from Kendall(defendant) stick was inadvertent and unintentional.
- Holding : If it appears that Kendall(defendant) was doing a lawful act and unintentionally hit and hurt Brown(plaintiff), then unless it also appears to the satisfaction of the jury that kendall is chargeable with fault, negligence, carelessness, or want of prudence.

  Accordingly Brown fails to sustain the burden of proof and is not entitled to recover. Brown, as the plaintiff, has the burden of proof as to Kendall's duty of care.

3. The Stand of Care[43)]

(1) Ordinary caution did not involve forethought of this extraordinary peril.

(2) If the defendant could have foreseen injury to particular person, she has a duty to him.[44)] If she could not have foreseeable the harm, there is usually no duty.

Some case easy. Suppose Glorious University operates a cafeteria. Does the school have a duty of due care to its dinners? Absolutely. Management knows that a grimy kitchen can cause serious illness, so the university has a duty to each of its patrons. On the other hand, assume the school bookstore sells a road map of Greece to a student. During spring break, the student drivers recklessly along a narrow country lane in Greece, injuring a farmer. The university could

43 Marc A. Franklin and Robert L. Rabin, Tort Law and Alternatives –cases and materials–, Foundation Press, New York, 2001, pp.37–42.

44 Korea civil law Article 393 paragraph 1, Article 393 pargraph 2 is same with american law.

never have foreseeable harm to a Greek farmer merely from selling a map, so it never had a duty to the man.

(3) In algebraic terms

<table>
<tr>
<td>In algebraic terms :
① Injury : L
② Probability : P
③ Burden : B
liability depends upon whether B is less than L multiplied by P : I.e., whether B〈PL
(Hand Formula).[45]</td>
<td>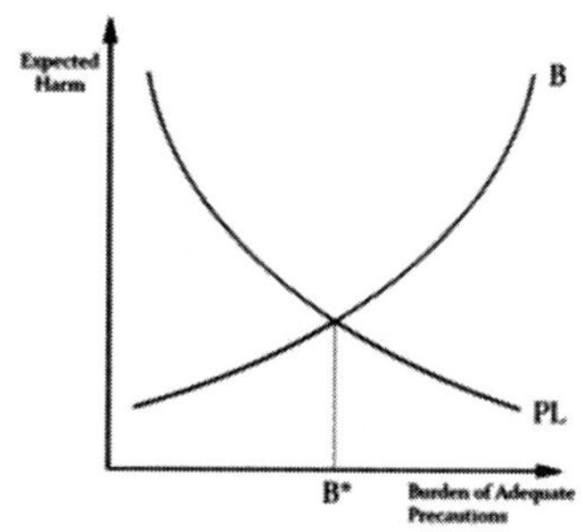
</td>
</tr>
</table>

If the probability be called P; the injury, L; and the burden, B; liability depends upon whether B is less than L multiplied by P : i.e., whether B〈PL(Hand Formula).

If the burden of adequate precautions is less than the product of the probability that a vessel will break free and the gravity of the resulting injury if she does (B〈PL), Liability would attach under the appropriate circumstances.

45 http://www.libertylawsite.org/book-review/incentive-engineering/

4. Negligence, The Reasonable Prudent Person[46)]

(1) In Bethel v. New York City Transit Authority, In Bethel was injured on the NY City Transit Authority's bus when an wheelchair seat collapsed. The Court recognized that, reasonable person standard is sufficiently flexible by itself to permit courts and juries fully into account the ultra hazardous nature of a tortfeasor's activity. Transit Authority is subject to the same duty of care as any other potential tortfeasor—reasonable care under all of the circumstances of the particular case.

Courts apply the reasonable person standard, a defendant breaches his duty of due care by failing to behave the way a reasonable person would under similar circumstance. Reasonable "person" means someone of the defendant's occupation. So the standard is always "reasonable", but what is considered reasonable can change depending on

46 Bethel v. New York City Transit Authority, Cout of Appeals of New York, 1998.

the circumstances.

(2) A taxi driver must driver as a reasonable taxi driver has a duty to do.

(3) In Casarez v. NME Hospitals Dr, Vasquez admitted to a hospital a patient who was terminally ill with acquired immune deficiency syndrome(AIDS). In his admission instruction, the doctor stated that the patient was HIV positive; he also told the nurses of the patient's condition. Casarez, a certified nursing assistant, was caring for the patient when the involuntarily spewed blood on Casarez's mouth, eyes, and arm. The patient died the next day. Casarez tested HIV positive.

Casarez sued Dr. Vasquez(among others), claiming that the doctor negligently failed to instruct him how to handle an AID patient. But, He had no obligation to instruct staff in special procedures for such a patient because all hospital staff were already trained. Casarez and all others knew precisely what precautions to take, and Vasquez was not liable.

5. In general Roles of judge and jury[47)]

(1) The lower court did err in assigning responsibility to the Railroad(defendant) for Goodman's(plaintiff) death as a result of being hit by a train. He must stop and get out vehicle. It seems to us that if he relies upon not hearing a train or any signal, and takes no further precaution he does so at his own risk and will be responsible for his actions.

It was Goodman's own fault that he did not reduce his speed earlier and come to stop. Goodman relied upon not hearing a train or any signal, and took no further precaution. He should have stopped & gotten out of the truck.

47 Marc A. Franklin and Robert L. Rabin, Tort Law and Alternatives –cases and materials–, Foundation Press, New York, 2001, pp.58–65.

(2) Case (Andrews v. United Airlines 1994)[48]

1) Facts

Andrews, a passenger on a UA flight, was injured by a briefcase which fell from an overhead bin. Nobody knew who opened the bin or what made the briefcase fall. Andrews claimed that the injury was foreseeable and UA didn't prevent it. The district court dismissed the suit on summary judgment.

2) Holding

① United Airlines did not satisfy its duty of care toward its passengers, Andrews(Plaintiff) presented the testimony of two witnesses.[49]

---

48 Andrews v. United Airlines(1994); United(defendant) argues that Andrews(plaintiff) presented too little proof to satisfy her burden. United says 135 incidents are trivial when spread over the millions of passengers traveling each year. Indeed, United sees the low incidence of injuries as proof that the safety measures suggested by Andrews expert would not merit the additional cost and inconvenience to airline passengers. It is a close question, but plaintiff made a sufficient case to overcome summary judgment.

49 To show that United did not satisfy its duty of care toward its passengers, Andrews presented the testimony of two witnesses.

㉠ First witness was that US's manager to inflight Safety disclosed that UA had received 135 reports of items falling overhead bins. So UA added a warning to its arrival announcements that passengers should use caution in opening the overhead bins because items may have shifted during flight.

㉡ Andrews' second witness was a safety and human factor expert, who testified that United's announcement was ineffective because passengers could not see objects poised to fall until it was too late to prevent it. He also testified that United could have taken additional steps to prevent the hazard, such as retrofitting its overhead bins with baggage nets.

② Defendant argued that Andrews presented too little proof to satisfy her burden. United Airline says 135 incidents are trivial when spread over the millions of passengers traveling each year. Defendant believed that this low incidence of injuries was a proof that safety measures suggested by Plaintiff's expert were not cost effective.

③ We conclude that Andrews (plaintiff) has made a sufficient case to overcome summary judgement. The case turns on whether the hazard is serious enough to warrant more than a warning. Jurors, many of whom will have been airline passengers, will be well equipped to decide whether UA had a duty to do more than warn passengers about the possibility of falling baggage.

A reasonable jury might conclude United Airline should have done more, it might also find that United did enough.

If a jury could make a rational decision either way on the record presented, summary judgement is inappropriate.

(3) In Role of Custom[50)]

In Trimarco v. Klein, The appellate court held that if there was a custom and usage at the time to substitute shatterproof glass, and even if

50 Trimarco v. Klein, Court of Appeals of New York, 1982.

that was a better and safer method of enclosing showers, there was no common-law duty on klein to replace the glass unless prior notice of the danger had come to klein either from trimarco or by reason of a similar accident on the building. Customary safeguards establish a standard of care.

(4) Role of Statutes

Mr. Martion(plaintiff) was guilty of contributory negligence in failing to have a light on the buggy as provided by law. The unexcused omission of statutory signals is more than just some evidence of negligence; it is negligence in itself. A statute designed for the protection of human life is not to be brushed aside as a form of words, its commands reduced to the level of cautions, and the duty to obey attenuated into an option to conform.

(5) Legislature did not intend that a statute enacted for the preservation of the life and limb of pedestrians(defendant) must be observed when

observance would subject them to more imminent danger. Therefore Violating a statute doesn't necessarily mean you have acted negligently. Need to look at the purpose of statute, and the particular situation. If you violate a safety statute, you are assumed to be negligent unless you can show otherwise(to more imminent danger).

6. Proof of Negligence

(1) Here we focus on the plaintiff's burden of proving that the defendant's conduct fell below the standard of reasonable care.

(2) Viewing the evidence in a light most favorable to plaintiff, It cannot be said as a matter of law that the circumstantial evidence was insufficient to permit the jury to draw the necessary inference that a slippery condition was created by jars of baby food.

The jar of baby food had fallen and broken a

sufficienct length of time prior to the accident to permit stop and shop's employees to discover and remedy the condition. Circumstantial evidence pointed to the fact that the store had "constructive notice" of hazard and did not clean it. They had a duty because customers were invitee.

(3) If the plaintiff has made out a prima facie case, it would be error for the Court to dismiss the complaint. Circumstantial evidence is not insufficient. If the jury verdict is deemed by the Court to be against the weight of the evidence, that Court's power is limited to ordering a new trail.

(4) To constitute constructive notice

To constitute constructive notice,[51)] a defect

51 2015고정1519 도로교통법위반(사고후미조치); 1. Fact: 새벽 시간대에 가로등이 켜져 있지 않은 도로에서 불법 주차된 트럭을 들이받아 차량 전조등 파편이 바닥에 비산되었고, 차량에서 흘러나온 부동액과 오일 등이 도로 위를 흐르게 되었다면 사고현장은 사고 발생 이전보다 더욱 위험한 상태가 되어 '새로운 교통상의 위험과 장해'가 초래되었다고 봄이 상당하므로, 사고를 일으킨 피고인으로서는 바닥에 비산된 파편들과 부동액, 오일 등을 치우는 방법으로 자신이 초래한 교통상의 위험과 장해를 제거하였어야 한다고 판시하였다. 즉, 'Constitute constructive notice'가 있다고 보고 있다. 피고인은 2015. 3. 1. 02:00경 위 승용차를 운전하여 ㅇㅇ시 앞 편도 1차로를 ㅇㅇ고등학교 방면에

must be visible and apparent and it must exist for a sufficient length of time prior to the accident to permit the defendant's employees to discover and remedy it. The record contains no evidence that any one, including Gordon(plaintiff), observed the piece of paper prior to the accident.

Thus, on the evidence presented, the piece of paper that caused Gordon's fall could have been deposited there only minutes or seconds before the accident.

7. Res Ipsa Loquitur[52)]

서 ㅇㅇ공원 방면으로 진행하였다. 당시 야간으로 전방 시야 확보가 쉽지 않았고 도로 오른편에 피해자 B 소유인 ㅇㅇ호 포터 화물차가 주차 중에 있었으므로 이러한 경우 자동차의 운전업무에 종사하는 사람으로서는 전방을 잘 살피고 제동 및 조향장치를 적정하게 조작하여 안전하게 운전해야 할 업무상 주의의무가 있었다. 그럼에도 불구하고 피고인은 이를 게을리 한 채 그대로 진행한 과실로 피고인의 승용차 오른쪽 앞부분으로 위 화물차 왼쪽 뒷부분을 들이받았다. 이로써 피고인은 위와 같은 업무상의 과실로 위 화물차를 리어램프패널 교환 등 수리비 451,361원이 들도록 손괴하여 도로에 비산물이 산재되는 등 교통장해를 야기하고도 아무 조치 없이 그대로 도주하였다. 2. Apply of law (1) 범죄사실에 대한 해당법조, 도로교통법 제148조, 제54조 제1항. 3.Holding: 피고인을 벌금 200만 원에 처한다. 피고인이 위 벌금을 납입하지 아니하는 경우 10만 원을 1일로 환산한 기간 피고인을 노역장에 유치한다.

52 Marc A. Franklin and Robert L. Rabin, Tort Law and Alternatives -cases and materials-, Foundation Press, New York, 2001, pp.106-109.

Normally, a plaintiff must prove factual cause and foreseeable type of harm in order to establish negligence. But in the case, a court may be willing to infer that the defendant caused the harm, under the doctrine of res ipsa loquitur.

Suppose a pedestrian is walking along a sidewalk when an air conditioning unit falls on his head from a third-story window. The defendant, who owns the third-story apartment, denies any wrongdoing, and it may be difficult or impossible apply for the plaintiff to prove why the air conditioner fell.

In this cases, apply res ipsa loquitur that the facts imply that the defendant's negligence caused the accident. If a court uses this doctrine, then the defendant must come forward with evidence establishing that is did not cause the harm. It applies Because, ① the defendant had exclusive control of the thing that caused the harm, ② The harm normally would not have occurred without negligence, and ③ It must not have been due to any contribution on the part of the plaintiff.

8. The Special Case of Medical Malpractice[53)]

- Expert testimony is an essential requirement in proving standard of care applicable to the defendant unless the lack of care is so obvious as to be within the layman's common knowledge.[54)]
- Any doctor with knowledge of or familiarity with the procedure, acquired through experience, observation, association, or education, is competent to testify concerning the requisite standard of care and whether the care in any given case deviated from that standard

53 Marc A. Franklin and Robert L. Rabin, Tort Law and Alternatives -cases and materials-, Foundation Press, New York, 2001, p.109-129.

54 의사가 설명의무를 위반한 채 수술 등을 하여 환자에게 중대한 결과가 발생한 경우에 환자 측에서 선택의 기회를 잃고 자기결정권을 행사할 수 없게 된 데 대한 위자료만을 청구하는 때에는 의사의 설명 결여 내지 부족으로 인하여 선택의 기회를 상실하였다는 점만 증명하면 충분하고, 설명을 받았더라면 중대한 결과는 생기지 아니하였을 것이라는 점까지 증명하여야 하는 것은 아니지만, 그 결과로 인한 모든 손해의 배상을 청구하는 때에는 중대한 결과와 의사의 설명의무 위반 내지 승낙취득 과정에서의 잘못 사이에 상당인과관계가 존재하여야 하며, 이때의 의사의 설명의무 위반은 환자의 자기결정권 내지 치료행위에 대한 선택의 기회를 보호하기 위한 점에 비추어 환자의 생명, 신체에 대한 구체적 치료과정에서 요구되는 의사의 주의의무 위반과 동일시할 정도의 것이어야 한다(대법원 2013. 4. 26. 선고 2011다29666; 대법원 2014.12.24. 선고 2013다28629).

C. The Duty of Physical Injuries[55)]

1. Individual Duty : Obligation to other of special relationship.

- In Harper v. Herman[56)], the fact is that Herman and Harper did not know each other before the outing. Harper dive from a boat into the water, only two or three feet deep. Harper asked Herman if he was "going in" and when Herman said "yes," Harper dove(dive) into the water warning. Harper hit the bottom of the lake head first, broke his spinal cord, and became a quadriplegic. Harper sued Herman, claiming that Herman owed him a duty to warn him that the water was too shallow for diving.
- the court hold is that, The affirmative duty to

55 Marc A. Franklin and Robert L. Rabin, Tort Law and Alternatives −cases and materials−, Foundation Press, New York, 2001, pp.130−157.

56 Jeffrey J. HARPER, Respondent, v. Theodor H. HERMAN, Petitioner, Appellant, Supreme Court of Minnesota, No. C0−92−196, 499 N.W.2d 472, 1993.

act to prevent injury only arises when a special relationship exists between the parties. Even if Herman should have known that Harper needed protection, Harper must still prove that a special relationship existed that gave rise to an affirmative duty to act. A special relationship is only found on the part of common carriers, innkeepers, owners of land held open to the public, and persons that have custody over another individual under such circumstances that the individual is deprived of normal opportunities of self–protection.

The court of appeals ruled in Harper's favor because it found that Herman knew that the water was dangerously shallow and under Minnesota case law, actual knowledge of a dangerous condition imposes a special duty to take affirmative action.

However, actual knowledge without a special relationship giving rise to a duty to provide protection is not sufficient to establish liability for negligence. Finally, under the Restatement, there are certain dangers, such as those posed by fire and water, that can be appreciated by any child. If a child can be expected to appreciate the danger of diving into water, so can a 20-year old adult.[57)]

- Farwell(plaintiff) and Siegrist(defendant) were spending time together socially. The understanding that if one companion is in danger the other will help if by doing so he won't put himself in danger is implicit in any social undertaking, and to find that Siegrist did not have the duty to seek medical attention or tell someone about Farwell's condition after he had been badly beaten and was laying unconscious in Siegrist's car would be "shocking to humanitarian considerations". In this case, the social nature of Siegrist's undertaking with Farwell gave rise to a relationship.

57 Ronen Avraham, tort preview note part I. Negligence, 2006, pp.25-26; Ronen Avraham, Leemore S. Dafny, Max M. Schanzenbach, The journal of law, economics & organization. vol. 28 no. 4, Oxford University Press, 2012, pp.657-686,

2. Duty of Broad

Con Ed(defendant) is not liable to a tenant of an apartment building for injuries sustained in a common area as a result of Con Ed's negligent failure to provide electricity. Although a contractual relationship is not a prerequisite to finding that a duty of care exists, the courts have a duty to protect a defendant from "crushing liability". Public utility only owes a duty to its customers. Can't expand this duty to everyone in the public. Needs to be a defined orbit for liability will get out of control.

3. Obligation to Control the Conduct of others

(1) Duty of reasonable care can be extended to a 3rd party if defendent has a special relationship with the victim.

(2) Such a relationship may support affirmative

duties for the benefit of third person. Ultimately, Tarasoffs'(plaintiff) pleadings establish the special relation that arises between a patient and his doctor or psychotherapist.

(3) An employer owes to third parties the duty not to misrepresent the facts in describing the character and qualifications of a former employee in a recommendation letter where making such a misrepresentation runs the substantial foreseeable risk that the third party would be physically injured.

(4) The general rule of negligent entrustment is that liability arises out of the combined negligence and of the car owner, who lends his automobile to the incompetent driver.

1) One who supplies an automobile to an individual that the supplier knows or has reason to know is likely to use the car in a way that would involve an unreasonable risk of physical harm is subject

to liability. The evidence makes out a sufficient prima facie case for negligent entrustment against Ace and Gardner as well as Willson(defendant).

2) To claim under the negligent entrustment theory, it must be shown that the entrustor knew or should have known some reason why entrusting the item to another was foolish or negligent.

3) Vince v. Wilson[58)]

① Facts : Plaintiff was seriously injured as a passenger at the time of an automobile accident, caused by Wilson's grandnephew. Evidence shows that Wilson knew that the operator for whom she provided funding to purchase a vehicle had no driver's license and had failed the driver's test several times. She communicated this fact to defendant Gardner, an agent of defendant, Ace, prior to the sale of the vehicle. Wilson was also aware of her grandnephew's alcohol abuse

58 http://www.casebriefsummary.com/vince-v-wilson-vermont-1989; Vince v. Wilson (Vermont, 1989) Posted on March 4, 2015, tortsTags:Torts Case Briefs.

and use of other drugs. Evidence suggests that the operator's inexperience and lack of training contributed to the accident which caused plaintiff's injuries. When the grandnephew got into a car accident that injured Vince, Vince sued Wilson, Ace, and Gardner(salesperson) for negligently entrusting an automobile to an incompetent driver.

② Issue : Is a person who entrusts a dangerous vehicle to an inexperienced driver liable in tort for negligent entrustment?

③ Holding : One who supplies an automobile to an individual that the supplier knows or has reason to know is likely to use the car in a way that would involve an unreasonable risk of physical harm is subject to liability. Therefore, Woman gave nephew for a car. She knew he was a drug user. She is liable for his accident.

4. Landowner owe a duty[59)]

(1) The common law applies special rules to a landowner for injuries occurring on her property. In most states, the owner's duty depends on the status of the person injured.

(2) There are three types of plaintiffs in premiss liability cases. Trespassers, licensees, and invitees.

1) Licensee

Privileged to enter by expressed on implied consent. Owner must exercise reasonable care or make conditions safe or warn visitors of danger. Liable only if ① knows or should know of danger, ② should realize unreasonable risk, ③ expects visitors won't see it on their own.

2) Children

The law makes exceptions when the trespassers

59 Marc A. Franklin and Robert L. Rabin, Tort Law and Alternatives –cases and materials–, Foundation Press, New York, 2001, pp.190–210.

are children. If there is some man-made thing on the land that may attract children, the landowner is probably liable for any harm. Landowner is probably liable if a child wanders onto her property and drowns, unless she has fenced off the dangerous area.

3) Invitee

Invited to enter for material benefit of owner. Or if you throw open doors and invite everyone. Owner must seek out dangerous conditions and make them safe or warn or latent defects.

5. Balancing test

(1) Fact[60)]

Plaintiff was robbed in the parking lot of a Sam's Club, owned by Wal-Mart Stores(Defendant). Plaintiff

60 Posecal v. Wal-Mart Stores.(La. 1999); Brief Fact Summary. The Supreme Court of Louisiana granted Defendant's application for a writ of certiorari, to review Fifth Circuit, Jefferson Parish, Court of Appeals' decision, which found Defendant liable for Plaintiff's injuries.

sued, contending that Defendant was negligent in failing to provide adequate security in the parking lot considering the high level of crime in the surrounding area. The trial judge ruled for Plaintiff. Defendant appealed.

(2) Holding

The Court recognized that, Under the balancing test, courts weight the foreseeability and gravity of harm against the burden imposed on business to protect its customers from the harm. The foreseeability and gravity of harm are to be determined by examining the circumstances of each case.

Although there is no general duty to protect others from the criminal activity others from the criminal activity of third persons, business owners have a duty to take reasonable care to protect their customers from the criminal acts of third persons. Totality of circumstances includes everything. Can be widely used, approach is the totality of the circumstances test. Compares prior incidents of possibility of harm.

D. The Duty of Non-Physical Injuries (Emotional Harm)[61]

1. Meaning

- Emotional Harm of old standard was that there had to be physical contact.[62] Today, we utilize the "zone of danger" test, or even foreseeability.[63] Under normal circumstances, Plaintiff must show the harm manifested it self in some way.
- A plaintiff may recover damages for bodily

61 Marc A. Franklin and Robert L. Rabin, Tort Law and Alternatives –cases and materials–, Foundation Press, New York, 2001, pp.261–301.

62 korea civil law Article 751 paragraph 1, is same with american law; 제751조(재산 이외의 손해의 배상) ① 타인의 신체, 자유 또는 명예를 해하거나 기타 정신상고통을 가한 자는 재산 이외의 손해에 대하여도 배상할 책임이 있다, Article 752; 타인의 생명을 해한 자는 피해자의 직계존속, 직계비속 및 배우자에 대하여는 재산상의 손해없는 경우에도 손해배상의 책임이 있다

63 Mhttps://www.youtube.com/watch?v=VAJG2H2gtqo&feature=youtu.be; 서울중앙지법은 서울시민을 큰 혼란에 빠뜨렸던 대규모 정전사태로 재산피해는 없었더라도 정신적인 피해에 대한 위자료는 지급해야 한다는 첫 판결이 나왔다.

injury or sickness that are the result of a reasonable fear if immediate personal injury instilled by the defendant's act.

2. Case of Emotional distress

Claims of emotional distress become more compelling when the HIV virus appears. At the Honolulu airport, several baggage workers discovered their hands dripping with blood that had leaked from a medical shipment. The blood tested HIV positive. The workers were distraught, claiming that because their hands had open wounds, their were at risk of developing AIDS.

The Hawaii court allowed their case to go forward, even though the baggage handlers had never acquired the disease. Because the blood was in fact contaminated, the workers' fear was foreseeable and reasonable.

3. Zone of danger

(1) Plaintiff was in zone of danger

A cause of action for the negligent infliction of emotional distress may be maintained where the plaintiff witnesses the death or severe injury of a close relative at the scene of the accident caused by the defendant's negligence. Finally, that the plaintiff be near the scene of the accident seems to us a necessary corollary to and involves the same policies as the observation requirement.

(2) Exception to Zone of Danger

A physical impact isn't necessary if special circumstances clearly would cause emotional distress. High probability of distress replace the "zone of danger" test in some places.[64)]

64 부산지법 2010가합 22135호(손해배상); 일조 방해행위가 사회통념상 수인한도를 넘었는지 여부는 피해의 정도, 피해이익의 상실 및 그에 대한 사회적 평가, 가해 건물의 용도, 지역성, 토지이용의 선후관계, 가해방지 및 피해 회피의 가능성, 공법적 규제의 위반 여부, 교섭 경과 등 모든 사정을 종합적으로 고려하여 판단하여야 한다(대판 2004.9.13. 선고 2003다64602). 위와 같은 수인한도의 기준에 관하여 우리나라 국토의 특수성과 협소성, 도시지역의 일반적 거주형태, 건축 관계 법령에 규정된 일조권 등의 확보를 위한 높이제한 규정 및 이 사건 변론에 나타난 여러 사정 등을 고려할 때, 동짓날을 기준으로 오전 9시부터 오후 3시까지 사이의 6시간 중 일조시간이 연속하여 2시간 이

E. Causation[65)]

1. If there are several possible causes of injury, the law requires the plaintiff to show that his injury was caused wholly or in part by the conduct of defendant.

(1) Causation is the scientific or physical link between the defendant's negligence and the plaintiff's injury. Causation Burden of Proof must be prove by the plaintiff.

1) A plaintiff must also show that defendant's breach of duty caused the plaintiff's harm. Courts look at two issues to settle causation

Was the defendant's behavior the factual cause

상 확보되는 경우 또는 동짓날을 기준으로 오전 8시부터 오후 4시까지 사이의 8시간 중 일조시간이 통틀어 4시간 이상 확보되는 경우에는 일응 수인한도를 넘지 않는 것으로, 위 두가지 중 어느 것에도 속하지 않는 일조침해의 경우에는 일응 수인한도를 넘는 것으로 봄이 상당하다고 보고 있다. 한편, 일조방해나 시야 차단 등 생활환경 침해로 인한 인근 주택 소유자의 정신적 고통에 대한 위자료의 경우 위와 같은 법리는 분명하고, 일조권침해로 인한 손해배상은 그 책임을 제한하여 시가 하락분의 70%와 위자료의 배상을 인정한다.

65 Multistate Legal Students, INC, PMBR part a-multistate specialist-, Multistate Legal Students, INC, 2004, pp.18-19; Marc A. Franklin and Robert L. Rabin, Tort Law and Alternatives -cases and materials-, Foundation Press, New York, 2001, pp.341-373.

of the harm? Was this type of harm foreseeable?

2) Factual Cause

If the defendant's breach physically led to the ultimate harm, it is the factual cause.

① Example : Suppose that Dom's Brake Shop(defendant) tells Customer his brakes are now working fine, even though Dom knows that is false. Customer driver out of the shop, cannot stop at a red light, and hits Bicyclist crossing at the intersection.

② Effect : Dom is liable to Bicyclist.

Dom's unreasonable behavior was the factual cause of the harm.

③ Think of it as row of dominoes :

The first domino(Dom's behavior)knocked over the next one(failing brakes), which toppled the last one(the cyclist's injury).

Suppose, alternatively, that just as Customer is exiting the repair shop, Bicyclist hits a pothole and tumbles off her cycle, avoiding Customer's auto. Bicyclist's injuries stem from her fall, not from the auto. Customer's brakes still fail, and Dom has breached his duty to Customer, but Dom is not liable to Bicyclist.

3) Foreseeable Type of Harm

For the defendant to be liable, the type of harm must have been reasonably foreseeable.

In the explanation above, Dom could easily foresee that bad brakes would cause an automobile accident. He need not have foreseen exactly what happened. He did not know there would be a cyclist nearby. What he could foresee was this general type of harm involving defective brakes. Because the accident that occurred was of the type the could foresee, he is liable.

(2) Substantial factor

Reasonable inference of causation can be made where the defendant's conduct is deemed negligent because it creates the particular risk of harm suffered by the plaintiff. The law of causation in Connection requires that the defendant's conduct have been a substantial factor in bringing about the plaintiff's injury. To meet the substantial factor requirement the plaintiff must prove that

- The defendant's negligence was the but for case of the injury
- The negligence was causally linked to the injury
- The defendant's negligence was proximate to the injury.

(3) Particularly, but for the causation may be inferred where the plaintiff's harm is one of the core risks created by the defendant's negligence. Ultimately, In cases where causation cannot reasonably be proved with direct evidence(like in the case), an inference of causation is permissible if the harm to the plaintiff was one of the core risks created by the defendant's negligence.

The reason the FDA does not approve the prescription of new drugs at dosages higher than those that have been subject extensive study is because all drugs involve a risk of unknown side effects, often exacerbated when the drug is taken excessively. Where causation cannot reasonably be proved with direct evidence, an inference of causation is permissible. All drugs involve a risk of unknown side effects, often exacerbated when the drug is taken excessively.

2. Joint and Several Liability : Multiple Defendants of Causation[66)]

(1) Joint and several liability acts to hold each of multiple defendants liable for the whole of the plaintiff's injury.

(2) Both liable of the harm caused. Plaintiff may go after each one separately or together to collect the full extent of damages. Thus, if two drivers cause a car accident which injures a pedestrian and both drivers are found negligent, the plaintiff

66 Multistate Legal Students, INC, PMBR part a–multistate specialist–, Multistate Legal Students, INC, 2004, pp.21–25.

could satisfy his entire judgment against either of the two defendants.

(3) Toxic Harms

- Where identification of the manufacturer of a certain product is impossible, market share liability holds a defendant manufacturer liable for a percentage of the plaintiff's harm caused by its product that is proportionate with the manufacturer's share in the product market.
- Where the actual Defendant is unknowable, courts have adopted a market share approach out of fairness to plaintiff.

3. Proximate Cause of Causation[67)]

(1) Generally

Proximate cause(one of the biggest misnomers known to the law) is a line drawn by courts in an

67 Marc A. Franklin and Robert L. Rabin, Tort Law and Alternatives –cases and materials–, Foundation Press, New York, 2001, pp.399–4110.

effort to reasonably and fairly limit the defendant's liability. Proximate cause has nothing to do with physical or scientific causation, rather, it is a doctrine which limits a defendant's liability to only certain harms.

(2) Unexpected Harm

A tortfeasor whose act, superimposed upon a prior condition of the defendant, results in an injury may be liable in damages for the full disability. It's foreseeable that you would cause harm, even if it's not to the extent expect.

- This rule rejects the limit of foreseeability that courts ordinary require in the determination of proximate cause.
- Thus, once the plaintiff establishes that the defendant caused some injury to the plaintiff, the rule imposes liability not merely for what were foreseeable to the defendant, but for the full extent of those injuries.

(3) Direct result

Even though the damage could not have been reasonably foreseen, the fire was a direct result of the defendant's negligent act. The cause of the explosion was the falling plank, caused by negligent workers.

(4) Unexpected Harm

A defendant is liable for only those consequences of his conduct that are reasonably foreseeable at the time he acts.

- A negligent defendant is relieved from liability where harm is intentionally caused by a third person(superseding cause) and is not within the scope of the risk created by the defendant's negligent conduct.
- If the harm occurs in an unexpected manner, Defendant is more likely to get off the hook. But this is still an exception to being responsible for only what's foreseeable. A defendant owes a duty of care only to those plaintiffs who are in the reasonably

foreseeable zone of danger.

F. Damages[68)]

1. Meaning

The plaintiff's damages in a negligence case are generally compensatory damages, meaning an amount of money that the court believes will restore him to the position he was in before the defendant's conduct caused an injury. In unusual cases, a court may award punitive damages, that is, money intended not to compensate the plaintiff but to punish the defendant.

2. Compensatory Damages

A jury may award compensatory damages.

68 Marc A. Franklin and Robert L. Rabin, Tort Law and Alternatives −cases and materials−, Foundation Press, New York, 2001, pp.679−725.

payment for injury to a plaintiff who prevails in a civil suit. The Single Recovery Principle mandates that the court must decide all damages. past, present and future at one time and settle the matter completely. Damages may include money for three purposes. First, to restore any loss (such as medical expenses) caused by the illegal action. Second, to restore lost wages if the injury kept the defendant from working. Third to compensate for pain and suffering.

If you or a family member has been injured or worse as a result of taking a harmful drug, you may be able to sue the manufacturer to recover for your injuries. Plaintiffs typically want to recover damages for medical expenses, past lost earnings as well future earning capacity, physical pain and suffering and even mental anguish. Personal injury claims for persons who have been seriously injured by prescription or over-the-counter drugs with dangerous and undisclosed side effects include defective product liability, failure to warn and negligence. Liability will be determined by the facts of your case and liable parties can range from doctors, to the drug manufacturer, to the pharmacy that handled the prescription. Contact an attorney who can examine the facts of your case and advise you if you are eligible for compensation.

3. Punitive Damages

While the purpose of compensatory damages is to help the victim recover what was lost, punitive damages are intended to punish the guilty party. Intended for conduct that is outrageous and extreme, Designed to "make an example" out of the defendant and Should deter others from doing same conduct and prevent this defendant from repeating actions.

Sometimes punitive damage awards are huge, but in most cases they are close to or less than the amount of compensatory damages awarded.

▶ MEMO ◀

Chapter. Ⅳ
CRIMINAL PROCEDURE

A. Overview Of Constitutional Law And Criminal Procedure In The United States

B. The Fourth Amendment : Search and seizure law

C. The Fifth Amendment's Privilege Against Self-Incrimination

D. Sixth Amendment : The right to counsel

E. Fourteenth Amendment : Dueprocess

F. Criminal Procedure

G. Entrapment

A. Overview Of Constitutional Law And Criminal Procedure In The United States

1. Meaning

Criminal procedure in the united states in governed by

- State Legislation
- State Judicial Decisions
- Federal Legislation
- Federal Judicial Decisions
- State Constitutions

2. U.S Constitution Bill of Right

(1) U.S. Constitution Bill of rights provides basis protections including the right to an attorney, the right to not testify, the right to confront witnesses, and the right to a jury trial, among others.

(2) Most of the criminal procedure issues are concerned to the Constitutional Law. Criminal procedure takes major part of constitutional litigation.

(3) The incorporation concept[69)]

- The Bill of Rights originally limited the actions of the federal government.
- Fourteenth Amendment, however, provided that "no state" shall deprive citizens of life, liberty or property "without due process of law". This language was interpreted to mean that provisions in the Bill of Right that were a fundamental, intrinsic aspect of due process were incorporated into the Fourteenth.

69 Charles H. Whitebread and Christopher Slobogin, Criminal Procedure–an analysis of cases and concepts, Thomson West, 2003, pp.4–15.

B. The Fourth Amendment
: Search and seizure law[70)]

1. Arrest the Suspect

(1) Arrest

When there is a probable cause to believe that a suspect has committed a crime, the police make an arrest. During arrest the police may conduct a search of the individual and begin to question about the alleged offense.[71)]

(2) Probable

1) Probable cause must exist for law enforcement officer to make an arrest without a warrant, or seize property in the belief the items were evidence of a crime. Example : pistols and illicit drugs in plain sight; a suspect running from liquor store

70 Charles H. Whitebread and Christopher Slobogin, Criminal Procedure–an analysis of cases and concepts, Thomson West, 2003, pp.17–180.

71 Multistate Legal Students,Inc, PMBR part b–multistate workbook volume one–, Multistate Legal Students Inc, 2003, p.17.

with a clerk screaming help. Probable cause has to exist prior to arrest, search or seizure, facts and circumstances within the officers's knowledge and of which they have reasonably trustworthy information.

2) Probable cause required more than mere suspicion

Probable cause is required to obtained a warrant. A person may be legally arrested if there is probable cause that he has committed or is committing a crime. arrest warrant.

3) What is an arrest warrant?

A judge's order to law enforcement officers to arrest and bring to jail a person charged with a crime. If police don't have a search warrant, police go to the somebody's house, police make a search, that search is illegal. So police cannot use evidence of that search.

4) Arrest without warrant

When the police observe crime, there is normally no time to secure a warrant.

2. Reasonable Suspicion[72)]

(1) Stop

1) Standard for stopping

Stop is not an arrest, thus there's no need of probable cause. However, officer must have a reason to believe that criminal activity is afoot(Reasonable suspicion). The degree of certainty required lies somewhere between "reasonable suspicion," the quantum of certainty required to justify a "stop and frisk"[73)] and "beyond a reasonable doubt" the standard of proof in a criminal trial.

---

72 Charles H. Whitebread and Christopher Slobogin, Criminal Procedure–an analysis of cases and concepts, Thomson West, 2003, pp.244–264.

73 See § 11.03(a) for a discussion of the reasonable suspicion standard.

2) As the Court held in the Terry v. Ohio, ruled that a person can be stopped and frisked by a police officer based on a reasonable suspicion. At the same time, the Court implies that a "Stop(temporary detention)" is permissible based on "reasonable suspicion".

(2) Frisk

Standard for frisk : Reasonable suspicion of arms. If police officers pull out a weapon while frisking, it is always admissible as long as stopping is reasonable. If the police find an evidence of crime rather then weapon, it is admissible in some cases.

(3) Particularized suspicion doctrine

- Defendant argues that the suspicion was not enough for probable cause. The police should have more freedom for board searches. Court said it was ok for the board police to search even though there was destructive search and there was no probable cause. This is an exception to the Exclusionary Rule. To enable government officials to establish effective border security measures, their ability to perform duties shoulded not be bindered by micromanaging courts. The customs inspectors actions constituted a routine border search, and particularized suspicion was not required. It strikes a better balance between individual right and governmental discretion.

- There are other areas where you don't need warrant and also you don't need probable cause. Regulatory searches such as border searches, airport.

3. Search Incident or a Lawful Arrest

(1) Purpose of the search : to ensure safety and to protect evidence from being destroyed

1) Arrest must be lawful

Otherwise, search incident to that arrest is also unlawful and evidence will be excluded. Time &

Place; Search must be at the same time and place with the arrest.

2) Reasonable time

The search that takes places has to be within a reasonable time of the arrest. The basic rule is that the search incident to arrest has to be within arm span of the person being arrested.

(2) Conduct Search

Even if Police suspects that She is using illegal for some treatments, police may not seize from it, because they are not described in the warrant.

(3) Arrest the Suspect

Police arrive and inform someone that she is under arrest. Police reads Miranda warnings. if so they take.

4. Governmental Conduct

(1) The Definition of Governmental Conduct

The 4th Amendment's proscription against illegal searches and seizures has been judicially construed to apply only to government conduct.

(2) Search and seizure rules apply only to government officials. If the search is undertaken by not police officer who is not a government official, the 4th amendment issues and the Exclusion rule issues do not arise because it's not a search for 4th Amendment or 14th Amendment purpose.

5. Search and Seizure[74)]

(1) The Definition of Search and Seizure

Both the public expose and the reasonable

74 Charles H. Whitebread and Christopher Slobogin, Criminal Procedure–an analysis of cases and concepts, Thomson West, 2003, pp.244–264.

expectation of privacy doctrines have been relied upon in analyzing seizures as well as search of evidence.

The Supreme Court has explained that probable cause to search exists when the facta and circumstance in a given situation are sufficient to warrant a person of reasonable caution to believe that seizable objects are located at the place to be searched.[75)]

(2) Expectation of privacy doctrine.

- As the Court held in the KATZ v. US, They adopted the expectation of privacy doctrine. The person using the phone booth had an expectation of privacy even though it was a public booth. The police obtained evidence in violation of the expectation of privacy.
- Trespass of property & Public Exposure : In the Katz case, the Court applied "Public Exposure" doctrine holding that words spoken in a public telephone booth overheard on

75 Brineger u. United States, 338 U.S 160.69 S.Ct. 1303, 1949.

an electronic eavesdropping device were constitutionally protected even though the wording of the 4th Amendment does not encompass phone booths and no trespass of property had occurred. "Reasonable Expectation of privacy" doctrine holding that the focus of the 4th Amendment should be whether one's reasonable expectations of privacy in the place searched have been infringed by a police action.

(3) Who can object to an illegal search? Suppose I am in my house. Police comes in to my house with out a search warrant. They look around and find some cocaine under my bed. They charge me in the crime. They want to use evidence. Do I have the right to do that? Yes, my house, my cocaine. I have a reasonable expectation of privacy.

(4) Less expectation in public space

Aerial surveillance is not generally protected by the 4th amendment. Anybody could fly over and see if they have an airplane, then Anybody don't have an expectation of privacy. if somebody are growing marijuana where can be seen from an airplane. So, aerial surveillance generally is not considered a search.

If something is in plain view, if it becomes into a plain view as a result of using a flash light, telescope, binocular. Under the old trespass doctrine, they would not have been considered searches because there was no physical entry into private place. Now with the doctrine of expectation of privacy, an enhanced hearing or seeing should be considered a search.

(5) Shouting Police, search warrant

- The interests violated by the abrupt entry of the police have nothing to do with the seizure of the evidence.
- The Knock-and-announce rule was mean to prevent violence, property-damage, and impositions on privacy, not to prevent police from conducting a search with a valid warrant.

■ The Supreme Court, the Fourth Amendment also requires that the warrant be issued by a neutral and detached decision maker. Additional requirements, not clearly of constitutional stature, have been placed on the execution of warrants by statute or judicial decision.[76)]

6. The Exclusionary Rule & Other Remedies for 4th Amendment Violation

(1) Can evidence obtained during an unlawful search and seizure be used in a state trial?

1) The Fourth Amendment

Citizenry protection against intrusion into their privacy… The right of the people to be secure in their persons, house, papers, and effects, against unreasonable searches and seizures, shall not be

76 Charles W.L. Hill and Gareth R. Jones, Strategic Management Theory, Houghton Mifflink, 2003, pp.76–77.

violated.

2) The Exclusionary Rule

Evidence that is obtained in violation of the Fourth Amendment is not admissible in a criminal rule against the defendant.

3) Genesis of the Rule

As the Court held in the Mapp v. Ohio(1961), Any evidence seized in violation of the defendant's Fourth Amendment rights must be excluded from state as well as federal prosecutions.

(2) The Scope of the Rule

- The Court concluded that the only purpose of the exclusionary rule is to deter illegal police behavior; regardless of concerns about judicial integrity and the like, the rule should not apply when it is unlikely to deter.
- All evidence obtained by search and seizures in violation of the Constitution is inadmissible in state court. Both deterrence of police

misconduct and maintaining judicial "clean hand" justifies applying the exclusionary rule to the states.

(3) The police's search must be based on a valid arrest of a valid search warrant. The general rule is that evidence is obtained illegally by a police that cannot be used in a criminal trial.[77) The purpose for the rule is deterring the police from engaging in unconstitutional searches and seizures.

(4) The Reasonable "good faith" Exception

- What does the good faith mean? Usually it means quite precise thing such as conducting a search based on search warrant even though the search warrant in not valid. Even though that search warrant is not valid(the Police is given wrong documents, wrong information) because it's not based on probable cause, the police's using that warrant and then finding

77 This rule was applied to the states in Mapp v. Ohip in 1961.

some evidence is OK and that evidence can be used in court.

- Therefore, Evidence may be used in the prosecution's case-in-chief when obtained by police action on authority of a warrant subsequently found to be unsupported by probable cause, provided that they had an objective good faith belief that the warrant was valid and issued by a neutral and detached magistrate.

(5) The Fruit of the Poisonous Tree Doctrine

1) Fruit of poisonous tree doctrine(developed by USSC)

Expansion of exclusionary rule.

2) example if the police obtains some evidence illegally and if additional evidence come from the evidence, the additional evidence also cannot be used. In general, the exclusionary rule extends not only direct products of an unconstitutional search and seizure but also to ancillary(or derivative) evidence that results from the illegal search.

3) Confession as fruit

Courts should consider several factors in deciding whether a confession is an act of free will

- Whether Miranda warnings were given prior to any confession or admission,
- The Temporal proximity of the illegal police conduct and the verbal statement
- The presence of intervening circumstance or event; and
- The purpose and flagrancy of the official misconduct.

4) Accordingly, when the police brought the defendant to the station house for an interrogation even though they had no probable cause to arrest him. After being given Miranda warnings. But, the confession deriving from this illegal detention should have been suppressed despite the police's compliance with Miranda. so, this evidence cannot

apply in the case.

5) As the Court held in the Fellers v. United States(USSC 2004), the absence of an interrogation foreclosed petitioner's claim that the jailhouse statements should have been suppressed as fruits of the statements taken from petitioner at his home. As the Court held in the Fellers v. United States(USSC 2004), It would be unconstitutional to admit at trial his incriminating in jail, because these were the tree is tainted, the fruits are also tainted.

(6) The inevitable Discovery Exception

- Evidence obtained illegally may be admissible in a criminal trial if the prosecutor proves by a preponderance of the evidence that the challenged evidence ultimately or inevitably would have been discovered by lawful means.
- In the Nix v. Williams the motivation of the offending officer is irrelevant to inevitable discovery analysis. When discovery of the

evidence was clearly inevitable, a good faith prerequisite would put police in a worse position than if there had been no police misconduct.

C. The Fifth Amendment's Privilege Against Self-Incrimination[78)]

1. Privilege Against Self-Incrimination

(1) Fifth Amendment

No Person shall be compelled in any criminal case to be a witness against himself…

(2) Defendants in custody "Custodial interrogation" is inherently coercive (Miranda). This coercive nature can be ameliorated only if there are following two

- The suspect is told he has a right to remain

78 Charles H. Whitebread and Christopher Slobogin, Criminal Procedure-an analysis of cases and concepts, Thomson West, 2003, pp.360-398.

silent that anything he says may be used against him, and that he has a right to an attorney during interrogation, at state expense if necessary; and

- The suspect "voluntarily and intelligently" waives his right to remain silent and his right to an attorney.

(3) Self-incrimination

- The prosecution may not used coercion to force a confession from a suspect. The suspect may refuse to answer any question that could be used to convict him.
- 5th Amendment, 14th Amendment, 8th Amendment No one can be deprived of life or property, it must to be Due process.

2. Confessions

(1) In the Miranda v. Arizona, the Court made the 5th Amendment the pervasive perspective

for evaluating statements of the accused. Since Miranda, the requirement that persons subjected to custodial interrogation be told of their right of remain silent has been the predominant focus of the Court. Desire to balance between protecting people against police misconduct and admitting reliable confession

(2) The Due Process "Voluntariness" Test

- As the Court held in the Fikes v. Alabama, In the totality of the circumstances "that preceded the confessions" deprived the defendant of his power of resistance. It will not lie of his confessions.
- As the Court held in the Williams v. US, Confessions obtained through the use of physical brutality and torture cannot be admissible under any concept of due process. Accordingly they can defense of the Confessions.

(3) Accordingly they can defense of the Confessions

obtained through the use of physical brutality and torture. It cannot be admissible under any concept of due process.

(4) Miranda and Fifth Amendment Analysis

The holding : two important components.

- A person subjected to custodial interrogation must be warned that he has a right to remain silent, that any statement he does make may be used in evidence against him, and that he has the right to the presence of an attorney, either retained or appointed, before and during questioning.
- A defendant may waive these rights, but only if the waiver is made voluntarily, knowingly, and intelligently will it render subsequent confessions admissible.

3. Double Jeopardy[79)]

(1) Under the 5th Amendment, a person may not be retried for the same offense once jeopardy has attached. The 5th Amendment… nor shall any person be subject for the same offence to be twice put. In Green v. US justice Black provided "the avoidance of repeated prosecutions rationale" the classic description of why the clause embodies a fundamental principle of justice.

(2) The "Same Offense" Prohibition

The "element" test : In the Blockburger v. US, where the same act or transaction constitutes a violation of two distinct statutory provisions, the test to be applied to determine whether there are two offenses or only one, is whether each provision requires proof of an additional fact.

(3) example, the defendant may ask the court

79 Beth Walstom-Dunham, Introduction to Law, Delmar cengage Learning, 2009, pp.534-537.

to rule that evidence of a prior conviction that occurred a long time ago should not be allowed into evidence at the trial because it would be more prejudicial than probative. If the motion is granted, then evidence regarding the conviction could not be mentioned in front of the jury, with out permission. "Whether jeopardy attached in the original state proceeding" an if so, whether the state court terminated jeopardy in a way that prevents reprosecution.

4. Federal Habeas Corpus

(1) Basic of Collateral Attack

- An error of federal constitutional dimension is alleged, the defendant either can petition the Supreme Court for direct of the alleged constitutional errors, or he can petitional a US district court to issue a "writ of habeas corpus" a collateral remedy challenging the legitimacy of the courts. The only realistic access to further federal review of state court decisions is through the vehicle of habeas corpus petitions to the lower federal courts.

- The US Constitution provided that the privilege of the writ of Habeas Corpus shall not be suspended.

(2) Procedural Considerations

1) Burden of Proof

The defendant petitioner must prove an unlawful detention by a preponderance of the evidence. Indigents have no right to appointed counsel.

2) Standing of petitioner

To bring a timely writ of habeas corpus the petitioner must be in custody. State Prisoners may seek a writ in either state or federal court, whereas federal prisoners may only in federal court. In seeking federal habeas corpus, a federal prisoner must show both cause as to why an earlier objection was not made and a resulting actual prejudice.

(3) Federal habeas Corpus for State Prisoners

Certain requirement must be satisfied before a state prisoner can bring a writ for habeas corpus in a federal court.

1) Violation of federal rights

The petitioner must show that the state detention is in violation of federal constitutional rights.

2) Relationship with double jeopardy :

The state may appeal the granting of a writ and the defendant may be retried for the same offense without violationing the prohibition against double jeopardy.

3) New evidence relevant to Convict's innocence has been discovered, it based upon the decision in Arizona v. Fulminante. As the Court held in Stone v. Powell, A major restriction on the availability of habeas corpus is that a petitioner who had a full and fair opportunity to raise a 4th Amendment violation previously in state court will not be permitted to seek a writ in federal court. The petitioner has received a full and fair opportunity to raise the 4th Amendment claim in state court.

(4) As the Court held in the Hamdan v. Rumsfield Hamdan's habeas petition, he must first be given a hearing to determine whether he was prisoner of war under the Geneva Convention before he could be tried by a military commission. accordingly he can held on the habeas corpus in federal district court arguing that he was being held without due process.

D. Sixth Amendment : The right to counsel

1. The right to Counsel at Trial[80)]

(1) Due Process Origins

In Powell v. Alabama(1932), the Court

80 Charles H. Whitebread and Christopher Slobogin, Criminal Procedure–an analysis of cases and concepts, Thomson West, 2003, pp.474–477.

established the constitutional right of an indigent defendant to the assistance of court-appointed counsel for the first time.

(2) The 6th Amendment Actual Imprisonment Threshold

As the Court held in the Gideon v. Wainwright, the 6th Amendment's guarantee of counsel for indigent criminal defendants was fully incorporated the 14th Amendment. In Baldasar v. Illinois, the Court held that an uncounselled misdemeanor conviction, although valid under, may not be used to enhance a later sentence beyond a term of imprisonment of 6 months or more.

(3) Counsel at other Stages of the Criminal Process

As the Court held in Gerstein v. Pugh, defendant held that the hearing for a post-arrest judicial determination that the arrest is founded on probable cause is not critical stage. In doing so, the Court addressed whether the hearing must be accompanied by the counsel, confrontation, cross-examination and compulsory process for witnesses.

(4) Waiver of the Right to Counsel

As the Court held in the Faretta v. California, a criminal defendant has a constitutional right to represent himself at trial once waiver has taken place.

(5) The Sixth Amendment right to counsel is triggered at or after the time that judicial proceedings have been initiated 'whether by way of formal charge, preliminary hearing, indictment, information, or arraignment'.

2. Michigan v. Jackson(1986)

The Sixth Amendment provides a right to counsel even when there is no interrogation and no Fifth amendment applicability. As the Court held in the Fellers v. United States(USSC 2004), the absence of an interrogation petitioner's claim that the jailhouse statements should have been suppressed as fruits of the statements taken from petitioner at his home. he can take of the Right to Counsel.

Therefore, Miranda Warning, Right of counsel and fruit of comments have been applied to in the case.[81]

E. Fourteenth Amendment : Due process[82]

1. Constitutional Source of Criminal Procedure Right : 4th Amendment(controlling federal government actions) and 4th Amendment by way of 14th Amendment controlling state actions. 14th Amendment "incorporates" some of the Bill of right, "Due process of law" is read to incorporate some of first 10 Amendments. History of Constitutional due process right is a history of the views of particular majorities of the Supreme Court.

---

81 Miranda actually combined consideration of two case: State v. Miranda, 98 ARIZ. 18, 401 P. 2d 721, 1965; people v. Vignera, 15.N.Y.2.d 970, 259 N.Y.S.2d 857, 207 N.E.2d 527, 1965.

82 Charles H. Whitebread and Christopher Slobogin, Criminal Procedure–an analysis of cases and concepts, Thomson West, 2003, pp.477–479.

2. The 14Th Amendment : The doctrine of incorporation

- The Due Process Clause of the Fourteenth Amendment has brought about the application of nearly all of the right explicitly enumerated in the Bill of Right to the states.
- Due process : a process that a fair and civilized judicial system should provide to individuals. In Mapp v. Ohip case, USSC held that the due process clause in 14th amendment applied the state criminal cases. The first reason is to discourage the police's misconduct. There is no other alternative way to discourage it. Second reason is Clean Hands doctrine.

F. CRIMINAL PROCEDURE

1. Pre–trial Proceeding[83)]

(1) Identification Procedure

1) Booking

This is an administrative procedure recording the arrestee. At the police station, the suspect undergoes certain identifications and evidentiary tests(photos, fingerprints, blood samples. etc).

At this stage, the suspect has no right to counsel or privilege self–incrimination. If minor charges are involved, the police may release the arrestee at this point. For serious charges, the person usually remains in custody and a more formal interrogation may take place. At this stage, the suspect has no right to counsel or privilege against self–incrimination.[84)]

83 Charles H. Whitebread and Christopher Slobogin, Criminal Procedure–an analysis of cases and concepts, Thomson West, 2003, pp.527–542.

84 Purpose of criminal Pre–trial Proceeding is that assist the police, provide rights to the police, provide an opportunity for the accused

2) Interrogation

Questioning of a suspect or witness by law enforcement authorities.

3) Lineup

A law enforcement method used in an attempt to have a witness or victim identify a person suspected of committing a crime.

4) Filing Complaint

After a suspect is arrested and booked, a complaint is prepared by the police or a prosecutor and is filed with the court. A complaint is a written statement of the essential facts constituting the offense charged.

(2) Preliminary Hearing

1) In felony cases

If the probable cause is found(when there is

---

to be released pending trial, determine whether a trial should proceed.

no arrest warrant), there is an arrest warrant, a decision is made as to whether the arrestee can be released on own recognizance, subjected to bail conditions, or detained preventively.

2) Gestation hearing

Preliminary hearing to determine Probable Cause to detain. An arrestee has a Fourth Amendment right to be released from detention if there is no probable cause to hold her. When the police arrest a suspect without an arrest warrant or a prior grand jury indictment, a prompt judicial determination of probable cause must ordinarily be made in order or continue to detain her where significant pretrial restraint on liberty is involved.

3) Bail hearing

The arrestee is entitled to a prompt bail hearing. A judge or magistrate will set an amount of bail that she must pay in order to go free pending the trial. The purpose of bail is to ensure that the suspect will appear for all future court hearings.

The Eight Amendment prohibits the setting of excessive bail.

4) Preliminary hearing to determine Probable Cause to Prosecute

Before filing an information or moving to the grand jury indictment proceeding, the prosecutor is expected to go through this preliminary hearing. This is an adversarial procedure to determine probable cause to prosecute. The suspect has a right to counsel at this stage. This is essentially a mini–trial with witnesses testifying and being cross– examined

(3) Grand Jury Indictment

- In some states and the federal system, the prosecutor must go to a grand jury to obtain an indictment.
- An indictment is a written accusation of charges against the defendant which a grand jury reviews to determine if the prosecution's evidence justifies a trial.

■ A Fifth Amendment right to a grand jury exists in all federal felony cases.

■ A group of citizens convened in a criminal case to consider the prosecutor's evidence and determine whether probable cause exists to prosecute.

2. Trial Procedure

(1) Arraignment and Pleading

1) The court informs the defendant of her charges and asks her how she pleads

2) Three Pleas

■ Not-Guilty Plea

When the accused pleads not guilty(or remains silent), a case is set for trial.[85]

---

85 Beth Walstom-Dunham, Introduction to Law, Delmar cengage Learning, 2009, p.561; The crucial stage of any prosecutions is the trail. At this point, the trier of fact uusally the jury will determine the guilt or innocence of the defendant based on the evidence of the prosecution

■ Guilty Plea

Upon a guilty plea which constitutes a waiver of a jury trial, the judge then determines if the plea was voluntarily and intelligently made.

■ Plea of nolo Contendere

A defendant may enter this plea, in which he does not accept or deny responsibility for the charges but agrees to accept punishment.

(2) Plea Bargaining

A defendant may agree to plead guilty to an offense in return for the prosecutor's recommendation for a lesser sentence or a dismissal of charge.

(3) Motion to Suppress

■ If the defense claims that the prosecution obtained evidence illegally, it will move to suppress it.

■ A "motion to suppress" is a request that the court exclude certain evidence because it was obtained in violation of the Constitution.

(4) Trial

- When there is no plea bargain, the case must go to trial.
- The prosecution bears the burden of proving[86] each element of the crime beyond a reasonable doubt.
- After the presentation of evidence, a verdict(finding of a jury in a trial) is reached and sentence(judicial decision of the punishment) imposed.
- The defense counsel will do everything possible to win an acquittal(Judgment that a defendant is not guilty of a crime as charged).

86 Beth Walstom−Dunham, Introduction to Law, Delmar cengage Learning, 2009, p.561; In the U.S. legal system , individuals are considered innocent until proven guilty. Furthermore, they cannot be compelled to testify about information that might incriminate them. Some defendants, regardless of innocence, simply are not effective witnesses in a criminal prosecution because they do not communicate well, and they do their defense more harm than good by attempting to tell their story to the trier of fact. For this reason, a defendant is not required to testify at trial. Further, a jury may not consider such a refusal to testify as evidence of guilt. Therefore, the evidence of guile must be established by the prosecutor.

3. Post-Conviction Issues

An appeal may be automatic or discretionary, depending on the level of the original trial court and the type of crime involved.

4. Conclusion

The U.S. legal system is committed to fairness to persons accused of criminal conduct, and every attempt is made to ensure that innocent persons are not convicted and punished. Much of the U.S. constitution was written with this objective in mind, and it continues to be the basis for all aspects of criminal procedure.

Criminal procedure begins at the moment law-enforcement authorities suspect criminal activity, accused individual are often afforded constitutional protections before they are even aware that they are suspects. An example of such a protection is the requirement of probable cause before any search, seizure, or arrest can be made.

When possible, this probable cause must be determined by a judicial officer who can view the situation more objectively than a law enforcement officer.

After a person's arrest, the Constitution continues to influence the proceedings through its mandates regarding bail, specific charges, Right to counsel, and a speedy trial. In spite of all these protections, innocent persons have still been convicted. In the majority of these case, however, the mistaken conviction occurred as a result of misconduct by witnesses or, in some instances, prosecutors. When properly applied, the system provides greater protection from improper convictions than perhaps any other legal system in the world.[87)]

87 Beth Walstom-Dunham, Introduction to Law, Delmar cengage Learning, 2009, p.564.

G. Entrapment

1. Predisposition Test

(1) The Supreme Court and the federal courts have adopted the predisposition test, Under the Court's interpretation of this test(or the subjective test). The two major competing interpretations of the entrapment defense are the predisposition, or subjective, test and the conduct of the authorities, or objective, test under the former, entrapment exists the defendant was not predisposed to commit the crime, Under the latter, entrapment exists the government conduct was such that a reasonable person would have been induced to commit the crime. then it will apply about entrapment.[88)]

(2) Some federal courts, and perhaps a majority of

88 Entrapment is often used in cases of prostiution and drug dealing. It is absolutely necessary for the police to do no more than accept or enhance the criminal conduct. The entrapment is that the police must plant the idea a person into criminal conduct that the person would not otherwise be predisposed to commit.

the Supreme Court as well, also recognize a due process defense, which leads to acquittal if the government conduct was outrageous. Although rare, some situations which might give rise to such a due process defense are :

- when police use physical violence to create and gather evidence of criminal activity.
- When the government supplies contraband wholly unobtainable from other sources or
- when, in a "criminal enterprise" situation, the government initiates, finances and exercises control over the operations of the enterprise.

2. Exclusionary

Minority view holds it should be construed as a constraint on police practices, As such, this defense operates like exclusionary rule to deter police engaging in particularly egregious behavior. Ultimately, Government should not be able to convict a person of a crime which the government itself instigated. Because, it has been applied of entrapment in the case.

▶ MEMO ◀

Chapter. V

BUSINESS ASSOCIATIONS

A. Partnerships

B. Agency

C. Commercial Law

D. Reality of Consent

A. Partnerships

1. INTRODUCTION[89)]

(1) Partnerships have two Important Advantage

They do not pay taxes and they are easy to form. Many professionals, such as accountants, licensed real estate agent and lawyers, have traditionally favored this of organization. Limited partnerships may be used as investment vehicles, where some parties are passive investors and other provide management and expertise. Some of the rules can be complex, however, and, like any relationship, a partnership requires careful tending.

Traditionally, partnerships were regulated by common law, but a lack of consistency among the states became troublesome as interstate commerce grew. To solve this problem, the National Conference of commissioners on Uniform State

89 William A. Klein and J.Mark Ramseyer and Stephen M. Bainbridge, Foundation Press, 2003, pp.92–110.

Laws proposed the Uniform Partnership Act(UPA) in 1914. Since then there have been several revisions, the most recent in 1997.

(2) Creating a Partnership

The UPA does not require partnerships to prepare a written agreement or make a formal filing. However, the UPA does permit a partnership to file a statement with the local secretary of state that contains basic information about the partnership.

The association of two or more persons to carry on as co-owners a business for profit forms a partnership, whether or not the persons intend to form a partnership.

Note that a partnership is an association of two of more people. If only on person is involve in the business, it is a sole proprietorship, not a partnership. Nonetheless, the court held that "갑" and "을" were partners because "갑" helped managed the business and shared in its profits.

(3) Difference of each Partnership

- Limited liability partnerships(LLPs) and Limited liability limited partnerships(LLLPs) are limited partnerships with no general partners. Have only recently been recognized by statute. Generally used for professional firms(lawyers and accountants) which were previously required to be general partnership.
- Each of these entities has familiar fiduciary duties, which may be limited but generally not eliminated. Flexibility does allow the operating agreement to permit competition.

2. General Partnerships

(1) Meaning

"갑" and "을" carry on the business together, sharing the profits and control. Partnership is legally presumed. Both "갑" and "을" are individual liable for all partnership debts. The Uniform Partnership Act of 1914(UPA) and the Revised

Uniform Partnership Act of 1996(RUPA).

(2) Formation and Dissolution

General Partnership may be formed automatically when two or more co-owners of a business share control and profits. No legal documentation is required. The partnership is dissolved upon the death, bankruptcy or withdrawal of any partner, unless an agreement among the partners specific otherwise.

(3) Financial Right

General partners share equally in profits and losses. Partners have no right to compensation for their service, unless provided by agreement. Firm's assets are distributed equally upon dissolution

3. Limited Partnerships(Limited liability Partnerships)[90]

(1) Limited partnerships, in their pure form, have

- At least one general partner which manages the partnership.
- At least one limited partner which does not manage the partnership, but has an investment interest in the partnership.

(2) General Partners

1) They are agents for the limited partnership

- Have authorty and obligations similar to partners in a general partnership.
- The limited partnership is liabile for their acts
- They have liability for the limited partnership.
- Unlimited liability for obligotions to limited partnership.

90 William A. Klein and J.Mark Ramseyer and Stephen M. Bainbridge, Business Associations, Foundation Press, New York, 2005, pp.61–63.

2) They have management rights similar to general partners

If more than one general partner(unusual), then they share as equal partners, subject to the partnership agreement.

3) Compensation

- ■ They may be reimbursed for expenses incurred on behalf of the limited partnership.
- ■ But, in the absence of a provision in the partnership agreement, general partners are not entitled to compensation for services performed on behalf of the partnership. In the usual case, the general partner or an affiliate of the general partner will receive compensation for services provided to the limited partnership, as specified in the partnership agreement.

4) Duties to limited partnership

- ■ Consistent with agency law, general partners owe duties of care and of loyalty to the partnership.

- These may be modified to a certain extent by the partnership agreement.

5) Fiduciary Duties of General Partners

- Default rule : General partners owe fiduciary duties to the limited partnership.
- They have a fiduciary duty to the limited partnership as well as to the corporate general partner. This is by analogy to trust and agency law.
- Thus, the directors of the general partner are liable, if they caused the general partner to breach its fiduciary duty, and if they are guilty of any self–dealing at the expense of the limited partnership.
- Can parties eliminate fiduciary obligations of general partner in partnership agreement? Current model statute say that parties may not eliminate duties, but may limit them and provide mechanisms for ratifying transactions.

(3) Limited Partners

1) No rights as agents of the partnership

- No right to bind the partnership.
- No right to manage the partnership.

2) No liability for debts or obligations of limited partnership

3) No fiduciary duty to limited partnership

Except duty of good faith and fair dealing in contractual relationships.

4) Liability of Limited Partners for Control

- Court held that their control over partnership mean that they were liable as general partners.
- Evolution of control exception
  - ▶Original position of courts : "control exception" A limited partner that exercises control over the operation of the limited partnership is converted to a general partner and then has liability for all debts

and obligations of the limited partnership from the time of his exercising control.

▶ Statutory limitations on "control exception" rule RULPA of 1976, §303(a); Limited partners control liability is only to parties that dealt with limited partner and reasonably believe that he is a general partner.

▶ The court holds, consistently with modern law that they are liable only if they actually were part of the representation of the client. And, because they might have been, they could be liable. consultation and knowledge about the case seem to be enough for the court to order a trial.

4. Limited Liability Companies(LLCs)[91)]

(1) LLC Fundamentals

- Owners of the LLC are called "members".
- Members have limited liability.
- LLCs can be managed either by its members or by a centralized, professional management(or through a combination of the two).

(2) Formation

- As with corporations, formation is a formality, involving only the filing of a basic form with the state(and a nominal fee).
- No minimum capital requirements, etc.
- Can be organized to conduct "any lawful business".
- State does not review operating Agreement(or Members Agreement as it is sometimes called).

91 William A. Klein and J.Mark Ramseyer and Stephen M. Bainbridge, Business Associations, Foundation Press, New York, 2005, pp. 64–74.

(3) Agency Law[92)]

- Under agency law, an agent's liability is discharged if the agent discloses the fact and indentity of the principal.
- Under LLC law, the members are not liable. One need not explain to creditors or others that members of an LLC have limited liability. But there must be disclosure of the LLCs status as such, by the use of "Limited Liability Company" or "LLC" in the name. Thus contracts should be signed(agent) for ABC, LLC.

(4) The Operating Agreement

1) The Operating Agreement in an LLC(sometimes called the Members Agreement) serves the same function as the articles of incorporation and bylaws serve in a corporation(or the partnership agreement serves in a partnership).

92 J.Scott Slorach and Jason Ellis, Business Law,−2015 · 2016−, Oxford University Press, 2014, pp.37−60.

2) It needs to cover issues such as the management structure, voting rights of members, and scope of fiduciary duties.

3) Note similarity to partnership here

It simply means that two parties are working together on a project. There could simply be a contract between the two, or there might be an entity, but that entity could be a corporation, partnership, or LLC.

4) Court holds that the Operating agreement holds

- The LLC itself is bound.
- The provisions supplant the provisions of the statute.

(5) Piercing the LLC Veil

- Claim against the owner of an LLC, which LLC had no assets. The LLC allegedly polluted land.
- Court, those principles can apply, in the right circumstances. The Model act says that failure

to observe formalities act says that failure to observe formalities imposing personal liability on members.[93]

- The Kaycee court says : "We can discern no reason, in either law or policy, to treat LLCs differently than we treat corporations".
- The piercing case turn on that Fraud, Commingling and Personal were involvement.

(6) Fiduciary Obligations

- Those fiduciary duties may not be eliminated, but the operating agreement may allow the members(or managers) to compete with the LLC.
- The Operating Agreement says : "Members may compete. Members shall not in any way be prohibited from or restricted in engaging or owning an interest in any other business venture of any nature, including any venture which might be competitive with the business of the Company".

93 Uniform LLC Act, § 303(b)

- The Uniform LLC Act says, at §103(b), says "The operating agreement may not…(2) eliminate the duty of loyalty under Section 409(b) or 603(b)(3), but the agreement may : (i) identify specific types or categories of activities that do not violate the duty of loyalty, if not manifestly unreasonable".[94)]
- There should be a test of reasonableness. The Court says that the duty of loyalty may not be eliminated.
- Under the court's interpretation of the operating agreement, it should be irrelevant. if there is a right to compete, then there is a right to compete.
- Court holds that Operating Agreement does not waive fiduciary duties or duty to operate in good faith. Self-dealing therefore requires application of entire fairness standard.

94 Bradford Stone, Unifrom Commercial Code in a Nutshell, Thomson West, 2002, p.21.

(7) Dissolution

- LLCs may be dissolved, just like partnerships and corporations.
- Creditors receive first priority, then members, pursuant to the Operating Agreement(or per capital).
- LLC has ended and has on assets.
- Plaintiff tries a piercing theory, but the court reject that because no evidence of fraud or other unfair dealings.

5. Corporate Law[95)]

(1) Corporate law still has its advantages. Rights and law obligations much more established. Management structures more established. Access to capital markets easier through corporations.

(2) The LLCs and corporations's same and different

- Corporations always have centralized management. Corporations presumed to have a separation between ownership and control(between shareholders and the board of directors).
- LLCs not presumed to have this separation. Indeed, more similar to partnerships in many ways, but with the intent of limited liability. LLCs designed to allow more flexible and informal operation.

95 William A. Klein and J.Mark Ramseyer and Stephen M. Bainbridge, Business Associations, Foundation Press, New York, 2005, pp.89–105.

B. Agency[96)]

1. Fundamental Notion

Agency is the fiduciary relation which results from the manifestation of consent by one person to another that the other shall act on his behalf and subject to his control and consent by the other so to act.

Many agents are hired for the primary purpose of entering into contracts on behalf of their principals. Salespeople, for example, may do little other than sign on the dotted line. Most of the time, the principal is delighted to be bound by these contracts. Sometimes the agent disobeys orders. As a general rule, however, the principal has no right to rescind a contract entered into by his agent.

The principal is bound by the acts of an agent if ① the agent has authority, or ② the principal, for

96 William A. Klein and J.Mark Ramseyer and Stephen M. Bainbridge, Business Associations, Foundation Press, New York, 2005, pp.1–5.

reasons of fairness, is estopped from denying that the agent had authority, or ③ the principal ratifies the acts the agent.

To say that the principal is "bound by the acts" of the agent means that the principal is as liable as if he had performed the acts himself. It also means that the principal is liable for statements the agent makes to a third party.

2. Definition

(1) Agent

1) One who is to act.

2) Elements not required for an agency relationship include

- A written agreement(unless the business of the agent requires a written contract).
- A formal agreement(acting like agent and principal is enough the establish agency).

■ Consideration(an agent does not have to be paid).

3) Agent's duties to principal

While the agency relationship exists, the agent owes the principal the duties of being loyal, obeying all lawful instructions and exercising reasonable care.

(2) Principal

1) One whom action is taken for

2) Principal duties may be specified in the contract between principal and agent.

3) A principal is liable on contracts made by the agent that are within the scope of the agent's authority.

4) Liability for tort

A principal is liable for the tort of his agent if

there is a master/servant relationship and the tort is committed in the scope of employment.

- A master/servant relationship exists when the principal has control over the "physical conduct" of the agent's duties.
- The tort is in the scope of employment if it is i) for the purpose of serving the employer ii) within the scope of the agent's duties and foreseeable even if it is an intentional tort.

(3) Analysis of Case

1) Fact

"A" lent her car to the baseball coach to drive to an away game; a crash ensued.

2) Issue

- Should "A" pay for the injuries in the accident?
- Was the coach the agent of "A"?

3) Holding

Yes. The coach was "A"s agent.

4) Rationale

- If he was her agent, then she is liable for his negligent tort.
- A manifestation of consent by one person(the principal) that another person(the agent). Act on the principal's behalf, subject to the principal's control and the agent's consent so to act.
- Because, "A" gave the car to the coach for a specific purpose and with a condition as to method attached.

3. Three types of authority

(1) meaning

A principal is bound by the acts of an agent if the agent has authority. There are three types of authority : express, implied, and apparent.Express and implied authority are categories of actual authority because the agency is truly authorized to act for the principal. In apparent authority, the principal is liable for the agent's actions even though the agent was not authorized.

(2) Kind of agent[97)]

1) Express Authority

The principal grants express authority by words or conduct that, reasonable interpreted, cause the agent to believe the desires her to act on the principal's account. Sometimes reasonable people might disagree about what the principal actually asked the agent to do. In cases of ambiguity about the principal's intent, the courts look at the principal's objective manifestation, not his subjective intent.

2) Implied Authority

Unless otherwise agreed, authority to conduct a

97 Business Associations, Foundation Press, New York, 2005, pp.6-7.

transaction includes authority to do acts that are reasonably necessary to accomplish it.

3) Apparent Authority

A principal can be liable for the acts of an agent who is not, in fact, acting with authority if the principal's conduct causes a third party reasonably to believe that the agent is authorized. Apparent authority may exist even where express authority does not, and even where express authority has been withheld.

C. Commercial Law

1. Secured Transactions[98)]

(1) Meaning

1) A model statute(Uniform Commercial Code) covering most kinds of commercial transactions in the us.

2) If the debtor defaults on an unsecured loan, whether evidenced by a note or not, what legal steps must the creditor pursue in order to recover?

3) Judicial Process

- Obtain judgment on the debt and Enforcement judgment using judicial process : Garnishment of receivables(including wages), Levy on tangible personal property, filing against other property of law suit, etc.

98 John F. Dolan, Commercial Law–Essential Terms and Transactins, Aspen Law Business, 1997, pp.91–106.

- Filling against other property(real estate, proceeds of law suit, etc).

4) Ineffective if the defendant is bankrupt, cannot be located or is otherwise judgment proof.

5) **A properly perfected consensual security interest**
- Allows creditor to foreclose on the collateral. Survives bankruptcy.
- Allows the creditor to take priority over later competing interests in collateral and over unsecured creditors.

6) Unsecured lending must rely on the borrower's reputation, trust. Lender only has to believe that borrower will pay back to have access to future loans. But interest rate will be higher. Loan of Contrary, Secured lending Promises to repay are backed by collateral. Lender can seize and sell the collateral if borrower defaults. Collateral may be real estate or personal property. Interest rate can be lower.

7) Two Ways of Loan Transaction

Unsecured Lending	Secured Lending
• Lender must rely on the borrower's reputation trust. • Lender only has to believe that borrower will pay back to have access to future loans. • Interest rate will be higher.	• Promises to repay are backed by collateral. • Lender can seize and sell the collateral it borrower defaults. • Collateral may be real estate or personal property. • Interest rate can be lower.

8) Function of Security Interest

In general : Facilitation of lending For lenders : Guarantee of paying back.

For borrowers Acquire loan otherwise impossible. At lower interest rate.

9) Article 9[99)]

- Article 9 of the UCC governs secured transactions in personal property.
- Article 9, revised in 1998, applies to any transaction intended to create a security interest in personal property or fixtures. About $^{1}/_{2}$ of all UCC lawsuits involve Article 9.

99 Bradford Stone, Unifrom Commercial Code in a Nutshell, Thomson West, 2002, pp.372-392.

- Article 9 Revisions : Throughout the past 10–15 years, revisions to Article 9 were recommended and adopted.
- Revisions include : Expansion of transactions covered, Clarification of rules for creating, perfecting, and enforcing security interests.
- Adoption of a medium–neutral provision meaning that security interests may be filed electronically, on paper, and in other forms.

10) Definitions[100)]

- Security interest : Interest in personal property or fixtures that secures the performance of an obligation.
- Secured party : Party who holds the security interest.
- Collateral : Property subject to the security interest.
- Fixtures : Goods that have become firmly attached to real estate.

100 Bradford Stone, Uniform Commercial Code in a Nutshell, Thomson West, 2002, pp.377–392.

- Debtor : Person who has some original ownership in the collateral.
- Obligor : Person who must repay money.
- Security Agreement : Contract which gives a security interest to the secured party.
- Default : Debtor's failure to pay.
- Repossession : Secured party's taking back the collateral because the debtor has defaulted.
- Perfection : Steps the secured party must take to protect rights in the collateral against people other than the debtor.
- Financing Statement : document filed by secured party to give notice to the public of security interest in the collateral.
- Record : Information on paper or other medium.
- Authenticate : To sign a document(includes use of symbols or electronic encryption).

(2) §9–203(b) Enforcement[101]

A security interest is enforceable against the debtor and third parties with respect to the collateral only if.

- Value has been given.
- The debtor has rights in the collateral.
- One of the following conditions is met : (a) The debtor has authenticated a security agreement that provides a description of the collateral.. (b) the collateral.. is in the possession of the secured party under section 9–313 pursuant to the debtor's security agreement.
- Therefore, Upon attachment the security interest is enforceable against debtor's collateral via foreclosure : self help or judicial process. If the creditor's security interest attaches when : Creditor gives value(loan), Debtor has acquired ownership of inventory of autos(collateral), and Dealer Inventory

101 Bradford Stone, Uniform Commercial Code in a Nutshell, Thomson West, 2002, p.394.

Security Agreement(Form 7.2) is signed.

2. Attachment[102)]

(1) §9–203(a) "Attachment"

A security interest attaches to collateral when it becomes enforceable against the debtor with respect to the collateral.

(2) Indication of Collateral & located

§9–504 Indication of Collateral. A financing statement sufficiently indicates the collateral that it covers if the financing statement provides :

1) a description of the collateral pursuant to Section 9–108; or

2) an indication that the financing statement covers all assets or all personal property.

102 Bradford Stone, Uniform Commercial Code in a Nutshell, Thomson West, 2002, pp.394–395.

- §9–502(a) A financing statement is sufficient if it indicates.
- Name of the debtor.
- Name of the secured party(or representative), and Collateral covered by the financing statement.
- The financing statement provides only cursory information sufficient to put third parties on notice.
- The financing statement should be filed where the debtor is located (§ 9– 301. §9–307) Defines where a debtor is located. A filed financing statement is effective for a period of five years after the date of filing. A continuation statement may be filed within six months of lapse.
- Limited filing in the real estate office is also contemplated(e.g., Country Recorder of Deed Office).

3. Perfection[103)]

(1) It will Perfection when The Attachment(Value, Rights in collateral, Security Agreement) and Notice(Filing of financing statement or secured party's possession of collateral, §9–310(a) "Except as other–wise provided", a financing statement must be filed to perfect all security interests) were combination. Perfection is basis for priority over adverse claimants.

(2) (a) §9–310(a) General rule : perfection by filing : [A] financing statement must be filed to perfect all security interest. (b) The filing of a financing statement is not necessary to perfect a security interest : … (6) in collateral in the secured party' s possession under Section 9–313. §9–313(a) Perfection by possession or delivery. [A] secured party may perfect a security interest in… goods, instrument… by taking possession of the collateral.

103 Bradford Stone, Uniform Commercial Code in a Nutshell, Thomson West, 2002, pp.402–422.

(3) Attachment and Notice

	Attachment	Notice
Non-Possessory	§9-203(b)(3)(A) Security Agreement	§9-310(a) Filed Financing Statement
Possessory	§9-203(b)(3)(ii) Possession	§9-310(a)&(b)(6), 9-313(a)Possession
Control	§9-203(b)(3)(B-D) Security Agreement	§9-314(9-104, 9-105, 9-106)

4. Remedies[104)]

(1) General

§9-601(a) Rights of secured party after default, After default a secured party may.

- Reduce a claim to judgment.
- Foreclose.
- Otherwise enforce the claim/security interest by any available judicial procedure.
- Proceed against goods or documents.

(2) Foreclosure on Receivable

§9-607(a) Foreclosure via notification of account debtor to make payments to secured party.

104 Bradford Stone, Uniform Commercial Code in a Nutshell, Thomson West, 2002, pp.512-520.

(3) Foreclosure on Tangible Collateral

§ 9–609 Secured party seizure of possession using either, Judicial process, or Self help if without breach of the peace.

(4) Disposition of Collateral After Default §9–610

Secured party may sell, lease, license or otherwise dispose of collateral.

Disposition must comport with commercial reasonableness.

- Secured party may purchase collateral if of a kind that is customary sold on recognized marker.

(5) §9–602(a). In the case of non–consumer goods, the secured party may accept collateral in full or partial satisfaction only if

- The debtor consents, and
- no timely objection from a person from a person of interest.

5. Perfection in Collateral

(1) § 9–317(a) A security interest··· is subordinated to the rights of : (2) a person that becomes a lien creditor before··· (A) the security interest··· is perfected. Therefore the security interest takes priority(and can successfully bring a replevin action for recovery of the autos seized by Foreign Auto Parts).

(2) Form 7.6 Installment Sale Contract contains

§ 9–514 permits assignment to be made in initial security agreement, and recording of the assignment. Assignment of perfected security interest need not be recorded §9–310(c).

(3) Hierarchy

	Method of Perfection
Chattel Paper	Filing, Possession(tangible), Control(electronic)
Instruments	Possession, Filing
Accounts	Filing

6. Proceeds of Collateral[105)]

(1) §§9−315(a)(2) [2] security interest attaches to any identifiable proceeds of collateral, (c) A security interest in proceeds is a perfected security interest if the security interest in the original collateral was perfected.

(2) §9−315(d) A perfected security interest in proceeds becomes unperfected on the twenty−first day after the security interest attaches to the proceeds unless, (1) the following conditions are satisfied.

1) A filed financing statement covers the original collaterl.

2) The proceeds are collateral in which a security interest may be perfected by filing in the office in which the financing statement has been filed.

105 Bradford Stone, Uniform Commercial Code in a Nutshell, Thomson West, 2002, pp.482−487.

3) The proceeds are not acquired with cash proceeds.

(3) The security interest in the proceeds is perfected other than under subsection (c) of this section when the security interest attaches to the proceeds or within twenty(20) days thereafter. Security interest does not have a perfected security on debtor's accounting goods unless it amends the financing statement to cover this type of collateral. The rationale for requiring amendment of the financing statement is that proceeds have no necessary relationship to the collateral.

7. Competing Security interests

(1) Main defaults on both loans

1) Fact

- "갑" Feb 1 $100k Loan to "을"

Security agreement conveys "갑" an interest

in automotive repair equipment. then Filed financing statement.

■ "병" Jan 1 $100k Loan to "을"

Security agreement conveys "병" an interest in automotive repair equipment. then Filed financing statement.

2) Perfection

- "병" Jan 1, "갑" Finance Feb 1
- Priority
- §9-322(a)(1) General priority rules
- Conflicting perfected security interest… rank according to priority in time of filing or perfection
- Priority dates from.. the time a filing covering the collateral is first made or the security interest… is first perfected
- First in time first in right rule. So "병" prevails, because first to file/perfect.

(2) Purchasers

■ Fact

"갑" : January purchases from "을" two cars for cash.

"병" : February 1 Security interest governed by Article 9. "을" dissipates proceeds without accounting to "병".

■ Perfection

"갑" January 1, "병" February 1.

■ Priority

- ■ §9−320(a) [A]buyer in ordinary course prevails if purchases 1) in fair, 2) in ordinary course from person in the business of selling goods of that type, and 3) without knowledge that purchase violates competing interest.
- ■ §1−201(9)··· without knowledge that the sale to him is in violation of the ownership rights or security interest of a third party in the goods buys in the ordinary course from person in the business of selling goods of that kind.
- ■ Therefore "갑" prevails, because §9−320(a) buyer in the ordinary course prevail.

D. Reality of Consent

When you signed the contact you did not truly consent because you lacked essential information. 'Problems in Creating on the Declaration'. therefore, in this section we look at the claims that parties make in an effort to rescind a contract based on lack of valid contract: fraud, duress and mistake etc.

1. Fraud Law[106)]

(1) Meaning

Fraud is an action that can be brought in a variety of situations, one of which is contract. Specifically, two types of actions for fraud can be brought to invalidate a contract. Fraud in fact occurs when one party tricks another into signing

106 Comparison with korea civil law § 110조(사기, 강박에 의한 의사표시) ① 사기나 강박에 의한 의사표시는 취소할 수 있다. ② 상대방있는 의사표시에 관하여 제삼자가 사기나 강박을 행한 경우에는 상대방이 그 사실을 알았거나 알 수 있었을 경우에 한하여 그 의사표시를 취소할 수 있다

a contract by leading the other party to believe the contract is something entirely different.[107)]

For example, "A" offers to sell "B" his house for $100,000, and "B" agree in writing to buy. After "B" move in and discover that the house is sinking into the house. You argue that when you signed the contract you did not truly consent because you lacked essential information.

(2) Requirement

Typically, these are four elements of fraud

1) A misrepresentation of a present or past fact that is false must exist.

2) The misrepresentation must be a material element of the contract.

3) The party making the misrepresentation must know that what he or she is presenting is false

107 Beth Walston-Dunham, Introduction to Law, Delmar cengage learning publish, p.438.

and also must intend for it to operate as an inducement to another to enter an contractual agreement.

4) The innocent party must suffer measurable damages as a result of its reasonable reliance on the misrepresentation.

(3) Effect

Both innocent and fraudulent misrepresentation permit the injured party to rescind the contract. In other words, the injured party who proves all three elements will get her money back. She will have to make restitution to the other party. If she bought land and now wants to rescind, she will get her money back but must return the property to the seller. If the maker's statement is fraudulent, the injured party generally has a choice of rescinding the contract or suing for damages.

If the seller's mistake was fraudulent, "A" will generally be allowed to carry out the contract and sue for damages. "A" could move into the new house and sue for the difference between what she got and what was promised, which is probably the cost of replacing the goods system.

2. Duress Law[108]

When a Duress by Threat Makes a Contract Voidable[109] : Restatement(Second) of Contracts §175
When Duress by Threat Makes a Contract Voidable: (1) If a party's manifestation of assent is induced by an improper threat by the other party that leaves the victim no reasonable alternative, the contract is voidable by the victim (2) If a party's manifestation of assent is induced by one who is not a party to the transaction, the contract is voidable by the victim unless the other party to the transaction in good faith and without reason to know of the duress either gives value or relies materially on the transaction.

The contract is also lacking when one party agrees to a contract under duress. If one party makes an improper threat that causes the victim to enter into a contract, and the victim had no

108 Jeffrey F. Beatty and Susan S. Samuelson, Business Law and the Legal Environment, Thomson Southwestern, 2004, p.324.

109 E.allan Farnsworth and William F. Young, Selections for Contracts, Thomson west, Foundation Press, New york, 2003, pp.213–214.

reasonable alternative, the contract is voidable. The key issues are thus whether there was in improper threat and whether the victim had no reasonable alternative.

Example, On a Sunday morning, "Hall" drove to pick up his daughter "B" who had slept at a friend' s house. But, "Hall" is like brutal criminal. so suspicious neighbor called the police, who arrived, aggressively prevented the "Hall", from getting into their own car, and arrested the father.

The officers took "Hall" to the police station for booking but eventually realized there might be some problems with the arrest, since neither of the "Hall" had violated any law or done anything wrong whatsoever. An officer told "Hall" that he could leave immediately if the signed a full release(stating that he had no claims of any kind against the police), but that if he refused to sign it he wound be detained for a bail hearing. "Hall" signed the release, but later filed suit for false arrest, false imprisonment, battery, and civil rights violations. The police defended based on the release.

The court held that the release was voidable because "Hall" had signed it under duress. The threat to detain "Hall" for a bail hearing was cleary improper because he had committed no crime. He also had no reasonable alternative to signing. Hall' s suit went to trial, where the jury awarded them compensatory and punitive damages, plus attorney' s fee, totaling over $600,000.[110)]

By contrast, suppose "A" slips and falls on some spilled soup in the restaurant. The restaurant owner threatens to sue unless "A" agree to pay $20,000. "A" signs an agreement admitting liability and promising to pay the money. Is the contract enforcement? if yes. Restaurant owner' s lawsuit would have been legitimate. and there is nothing improper about his threat. A threat to file a lawsuit is only improper where there is no basic for the suit and its only purpose would be to harass.

110 Hall. Ochs, 817 F2d 920, U.S. App. LEXIS 5822, 1st Cr. 1987.

When a Threat is Improper : Restatement(Second) of Contracts §176
(1) A threat is improper if (a) what is threatened is a crime or a tort, or the threat itself would be a crime or a tort if it resulted in obtaining property. (b) what is threatened is a criminal prosecution (c) what is threatened is the use of civil process and the threat is made in bad faith, or (d) the threat is a breach of the duty of good faith and fair dealing under a contract with the recipient (2) A threat is improper if the resulting exchange is not on fair terms, and (a) the threaten act would harm the recipient and would not significantly benefit the party making the threat, (b) the effectiveness of the threat in inducing the manifestation of assent is significantly increased by prior unfair dealing by the party making the threat, or (c) what is threatened is otherwise a use of power for illegitimate ends.

3. Mistake Law[111)]

(1) Meaning[112)]

111 Jeffrey F. Beatty and Susan S. Samuelson, op. cit, pp.321~324; E. Allan farn sworth and Willlam F. young, Selections for contracts, Thomson west, Foundation Press, New York, 2003,pp.141~142; Claud D. Rhhwer and Anthony M. Skrocki, Contracts, West Group, 2002, pp.289~296.

112 Comparison with korea civil law § 제109조(착오로 인한 의사표시) ①의사표시는 법률행위의 내용의 중요부분에 착오가 있는 때에는 취소할 수 있다. 그러나

A mistake is a belief that is not in accord with the facts.[113] Mistake means something wrong unintentionally. Mistake of fact occur when the person commits the act while reasonably believing something that was not true.[114]

It may be a basic error about the quality of the thing being sold, as both parties had made a mistake and that the contract was voidable. Some mistakes lead to voidable contract, others create enforceable deals. As used in the law of contracts, the term "mistake" refers to a belief that is not in accord with the facts. It is simply the first step in establishing a right to avoid or reform a contract.

Assume that a party contract to move a pile of dirt for a certain price thinking that the pile contains 700 yards of dirt. But if the pile in fact contains 1,000 yards of dirt. there was a mistake of fact. This may not be sufficient to excuse performance, but there is a mistake of

---

그 착오가 표의자의 중대한 과실로 인한 때에는 취소하지 못한다.

113 Restatement(Second) of Contracts §151(Mistake Defined)

114 Beth Walstom-Dunham, Introduction to Law, Delmar cengage Learning, 2009, p.520.

fact. If there is in fact only 700 yards of dirt but the actual price of moving the dirt exceeds the contract price, there is no mistake of fact.

The distinction is between bilateral(mutual) and unilateral mistake.

(2) Bilateral Mistake

1) Meaning

Restatement section 152 provision in part: When Mistake of both parties makes a Contract Voidable. If the parties contract based on an important factual error, the contract is voidable by the injured party. example, “A” and “B” were both wrong about milk cows's reproductive ability, and the error was basic enough to cause a tenfold difference in price. “B”, the injured party was entitled to rescind the contract. Note that the error must be factual.

2) Requirement[115)]

Where a mistake of both parties at the time a contract was made as to a basic assumption on which the contract was made had has a material effect on the agreed exchange of performances, the contract is voidable by the adversely affected party unless he bears the risk of the mistake under the rule stated in § 154.[116)]

The Requirement(elements) are involved in this statement and each is important.

① A mistake must relate to facts that exist at the time the contract is made.

② The mistake must relate to a basic assumption upon which the contract was made.

③ To Provided a basic for relief, the mistake must have a material effect upon the agreed exchange. Mistakes as to facts that have a

---

115 Claud D. Rhhwer and Anthony M. Skrocki, Contracts, West Group, 2002, pp.290~292.

116 Restatement(Second) of Contracts §152(1).

relatively minor impact on the transaction cannot serve as a defense or a basic for contract reformation.

④ The party seeking relief must not have assumed the risk of this mistake.

When a Party Bears the Risk of a Mistake: Restatement(Second) of Contracts §154
A Party bears the risk of a mistake when: 1) The risk is allocated to him by agreement of the parties, or 2) he is aware, at the time the contract is made, that he has only limited knowledge with respect to the facts to which the mistake relates but treats his limited knowledge as sufficient, or 3) the risk is allocated to him by the court on the ground that it is reasonable in the circumstances to do so.

3) Effect

This effect are involved in this statement[117]. In determining whether the mistake has a material effect on the agreed exchange of performance, account is taken of any relief by way of reformation, restitution, or otherwise which is

117 Restatement(Second) of Contracts §152(2)

covered in section 'E. Common Law Remedies'.

(3) Unilateral mistake

Unilateral mistake contract: Restatement(Second) of Contracts §153
Where a mistake of one party at the time a contract was made as to a basic assumption on which he made the contract has a material effect on the agreed exchanged of performances that is adverse to him, the contract is voidable by him if he does not bear the risk of the mistake under the rule stated in §154, and (a) the effect of the mistake is such that enforcement of the contract would be unconscionable, or (b) the other party had reason to know of the mistake of the mistake or his fault caused the mistake.

1) Meaning

This subject deals with a situation in which only one of the parties was mistake. The first question one might pursue is whether the other party induced the mistake.

Unilateral is that one party enters a contract under a mistaken assumption, a situation called unilateral contract. In these cases it is more difficult for the injured party to rescind a contract. To rescind for unilateral mistake, a party must demonstrate that she entered the contract because of a basic factual error and that either ① enforcing the contract would be unconscionable or, ② the non mistaken party knew of the error.[118)] Eexample, "A" sues "B", whose bad driving caused an accident, and army, who owned the car that "B" was operating. While the case is pending, Army' s insurance company "C" pays "A" a $500,000 settlement. Later, the state's supreme court rules that "B" was an unauthorized driver and an owner' s insurer is never liable in such case. "C" seeks to rescind its settlement, claiming unilateral mistake as to its liability. The company loses. "C" was aware that an appellate ruling might establish new precedent. The insurer settled based on a decision calculated to minimize its risk.[119)]

2) Requirement

---

118 Restatement(Second) of Contracts §153.

119 See, e.g, AID Hawai'i Inc. v, Bateman, 82, Haw. 453,923 P.2d.395, Haw, 1996.

In order to obtain relief for unilateral mistake, a party must first prove each of the four Requirement(elements) required for mutual(Bilateral) mistake as set forth in section '(2) Bilateral Mistake' above.

This includes proof that

① the mistake relates to fact existing when the contract is made;

② he mistake involves a basic assumption upon which the contract was made;

③ the mistake produces a material effect upon the agreed exchanged, and,

④ the mistaken party did not assume or legally bear the risk as to the mistaken fact

In addition, to obtain relief on the basic of unilateral mistake, one must also prove either, that ① the other party knew or had reason to know of the mistake, or that ② the resulting contract is unconscionable.

3) Effect

This effect are same as bilateral mistake,

involved in this statement.

① Effect of Fault of Party Seeking Relief: A mistaken party's fault in failing to know or discover the facts before making the contact does not bar him from avoidance or reformation under the rules stated in this chapter, unless his fault amounts to a failure to act in good faith and in accordance with reasonable standards of fair dealing.[120)]

Restitution When contract Is Voidable: Restatement(Second) of Contracts§ 376
A party who has avoided a contract on the ground of lack capacity, mistake, misrepresentation, duress, under influence or abuse of a fiduciary relation is entitled to restitution for any benefit that he has conferred on the other party by way of part performance or reliance.

② Relief Including Restitution: In any case governed by the rules stated in this chapter, either party may have a claim for relief including restitution under the rules stated in § 376.

120 Restatement(Second) of Contracts §157.

4. Conclusion[121)]

An agreement between two parties may not be enough to make a contract enforceable. Fraud, Mistake and duress all indicate that at least burden of good faith negotiating on the party in the stronger position. Do not bargain for a contract that is too good to be true.

Fraud is grounds for disaffirming a contract. The injured party must prove that A false statement of fact, Fraud or materiality and Justifiable reliance.

Mistake in a case bilateral mistake, either party may rescind the contract. In a case of unilateral mistake, injured party may rescind only upon a showing that enforcement would be unconscionable or that the other party knew of her mistake.

Duress is that if one party makes an improper threat that causes the victim to enter into a contract. The victim had no reasonable alternative, the contract is voidable.

---

121 Jeffrey F. Beatty and Susan S. Samuelson, op. cit, p.328.

▶ MEMO ◀

Chapter. VI

STRATEGIC MANAGEMENT

A. Overview Of Strategic Management

B. Analysis of Internal and External Environment

C. Business Strategy

D. Corporate Strategy

A. Overview of Strategic Management[122)]

1. Introduction

(1) What is a "strategy".?

1) Strategy is the determination of the long run goals and objectives of an enterprise, and the adoption of courses of action and the allocation of resources necessary for carrying out these goals.

2) Competition is a good Problem. It is not the strongest of the species that survives, not the most intelligent, but the one most responsive to change.[123)]

Opening case; In the last years Samsung, based in Seoul, Korea, has risen to become the most profitable consumer electronics company in the world Since 1999 its revenues have doubled, and in 2004 it made a record $ 12billion profit,

122 Charles W.L. Hill and Gareth R. Jones, Strategic Management Theory, Houghton Mifflink, 2003, pp.2-11.

123 Charles Darwin.

thus becoming the second most profitable global technology company after Microsoft. The story of how Samsung's business model has changed over time explains how the company has reached its enviable position. In the 1980s, Samsung watched as Japanese companies like Sony and Matsushita(the maker of Panasonic and JVC products). Then Samsung's engineers would find ways to imitate this technology, just as Japanese companies had imitated U.S. electronics companies in the 1950s when they were the world's leading electronics makers. Samsung would make a low-cost copy of these products and sell them at lower prices than Japanese companies. Samsung continued to pursue its low-cost strategy the mid 1990s, when its chairman, Lee Kun Hee, made a major decision. Sensing the emerging threat posed by China and other Asian countries whose cheap labor would rob Samsung of its low-cost advantage. The question was how to this, given that companies like Sony, Panasonic were leader in electronics research and development. Lee began his new strategy by closing down thirty−two unprofitable product divisions and laying off 40 percent of Samsung's work force. Having lowered its cost structure and could now invest much more of its capital in research and development activities. Today, Samsung is a major supplier of chips and LCD screens to all global electronics makers, and it can produce these components at a much lower cost than they can because it is farther down the experience curve. Moreover, today Samsung is not just imitating sony's leading−edge technology but is also developing its own, as shown by the fact that in 2004 Sony and Samsung announced a major agreement to share the costs of basic research into improving LCDs, which run into billions of dollars. Samsung is relying on the speed of its research and engineering to fight off their challenge, but all global electronics makes are now in a race to speed their products to market.[124)]

---

124 Charles W.L. Hill and Gareth R. Jones, Strategic Management Theory, Houghton Mifflink, 2003, pp.149−150.

3) The major components of the strategic management process are defining the mission, vision and major goals of the organization; analyzing the external and internal environments of the organization; choosing a business model and strategies that align an organization's strengths and weaknesses with external environmental opportunities and threats; and adopting organizational structures and control systems to implement the organization's chosen strategies.

(2) Major Contents

1) Strategy Formulation

Strategy formulation is the process by which managers select and then implement a set of strategies that aim to achieve a competitive advantage. Strategy formulation is the task of selecting strategies.

- Corporate Vision and Goals
- External Analysis
- Internal Analysis

- Business Strategy
- Corporate Strategy

2) Strategy Implementation

Strategy implementation is the task of putting strategies into action, which includes designing, delivering, and supporting products.

(3) Strategic Managers

1) Functional Level Managers

Functional managers, who are responsible for supervising a particular function, that is, a task, activity, or operation, such as accounting, marketing, R&D, information technology, or logistics.

- Functional managers provided most of the information that makes it possible for business and corporate-level general managers to formulate realistic and attainable strategies. Indeed, because they are closer to the customer than the typical general manager is, functional managers themselves may generate important ideas that subsequently may become major strategies for the company.

- Thus, it is important for general managers listen closely to the ideas of their functional mangers.

2) Business Level Managers

Usually responsible for the translation of strategic direction and strategic intent from the corporate-level into strategies at the business-level.

3) Corporate Strategy

Chief executive officer would usually be responsible for

- defining mission and goals.
- determining what business the organization should be in.
- allocating resources among different businesses.
- formulating and implementing strategies that

span more than one business.

2. The Strategy Making Process[125)]

(1) We can now turn our attention to the process by which managers formulate and implement strategies.

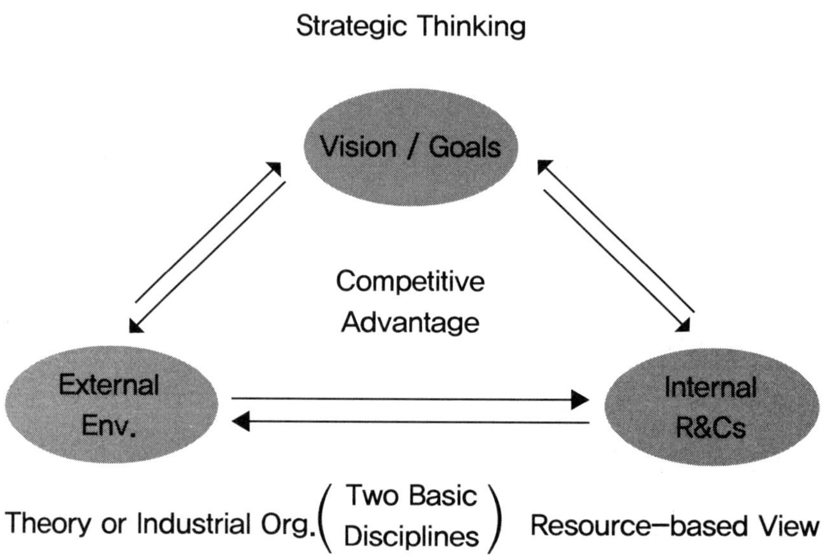

(2) A model of the Strategic planing Process : The formal strategic planning process has five steps.

125 Charles W.L. Hill and Gareth R. Jones, Strategic Management Theory, Houghton Mifflink, 2003, pp.11–13.

1) Select the corporate mission and major corporate goals.

2) Analyze the organization's external competitive environment to identify opportunities and threats.

3) Analyze the organization's internal operating environment to identify the organization's strengths and weaknesses.

4) Select strategies that build on the organization's strengths and correct its weaknesses in order to take advantage of external opportunities and counter external threats. These strategies should be consistent with the mission and major goals of the organization. They should be congruent and constitute a viable business model.

5) Implement the strategies.

B. Analysis of Internal and External Environment[126)]

1. Swot Analysis and the Business Model[127)]

The comparison of strengths, weaknesses and its external opportunities and threats. The comparison of strengths, weaknesses, opportunities, and threats is normally referred to as a SWOT analysis. Its central purpose is to identify the strategies that will create a company–specific business model that will best align, match a company's resources and capabilities to the demands of the environment in which it operates.

In essence a SWOT analysis is a methodology for choosing between competing business models and for fine–tuning the business model that managers chose.

126 Michael A. Hitt and R. Duane Ireland and Robert E. Hoskisson, Strategic Management, Thomas Southwestern, 2005, pp.34–68.

127 Charles W.L. Hill and Gareth R. Jones, Strategic Management Theory, Houghton Mifflink, 2003, pp.19–20.

2. Internal Analysis

(1) Internal analysis is concerned with identifying the strengths and weaknesses of the company.

(2) Internal analysis is a three-step process.[128)]

How to Complete a SWOT Analysisa		
	Strengths	Weaknesses
Internal	• Positive brand recognition • Intellectual property • Cost advantages • Skilled workforce • Financial resources	• Negative brand recognition • Expiring intellectual property • Rising costs • Unskilled workforce • Lack of financial resources
	Opportunities	Threats
External	• New technology • Relaxing government regulations • Elimination of international trade barriers • Changing consumer preference	• Emergence of new competitors • Pending government regulations • Increased trade barriers • Pending lawsuits • New technology

128 Charles W.L. Hill and Gareth R. Jones, Strategic Management Theory, Houghton Mifflink, 2003, pp.76–77.

- A SWOT analysis is a simple but widely used tool that helps in understanding the strengths, weaknesses, opportunities and threats involved in a project, life plan or business activity.
- Tool used to complete an objective analysis of a company
- Helps identify both sources of competitive advantages as well as potential liabilites
- Also useful when evaluating the investment worthiness of a company

1) Managers must understand the process by which companies create value for customers and profit for themselves, and they need to understand the role of resources, capabilities, and distinctive competencies in the process.

2) They need to understand how important superior efficiency, innovation, quality and responsiveness to customers are in creating value and generating high profitability.

3) They must be able to analyze the ability of their company's competitive advantage to identify what is driving the profitability of their enterprise and where opportunities for improvement might lie.

(3) Resources and Capabilities

1) In order to achieve a competitive advantage, a company needs to pursue strategies that build on its existing resources and capabilities and formulate strategies that build additional resources and capabilities. The source of a competitive advantage is superior value creation. To create superior value, a company must lower its costs or differentiate its product so that it creates more value and can charge a higher price.

2) Resources

- Capital or financial, physical, social or human, technological, and organizational factor endowments.
- A firm-specific and difficult to imitate resource is likely to lead to distinctive competencies.

3) Capabilities

- A company's skills at coordinating and using

its resources.

- Capabilities are the product of organizational structure, processes, and control systems.

(4) The Durability of Competitive Advantage

1) The Durability of a company's competitive advantage depends on the height of barriers to imitation, the capability of competitors, and environmental dynamism.

2) Sustaining Competitive Advantage : Develop distinctive competencies and superior performance in efficiency, quality, Innovation and responsiveness to Customers.

(5) A Framework for Analyzing R & Cs

1) Identify the firm's R & Cs.

2) Explore the linkages between R & Cs.

3) Appraise the firm's R & Cs in terms of strategic importance and relative strength.

4) Develop strategy implications in relation to strengths : We can these be exploited more effectively and fully.

5) Develop strategy implication in relation to weaknesses.

- Identify opportunities to outsourcing activities that can be better performed by other organizations.
- We can weaknesses be corrected through acquiring and developing R & Cs.

6) The ability of a company to attain superior efficiency, quality, innovation and customer responsiveness will determine if its product offering is differentiated from that of rivals and if it has a low cost structure.

3. External Analysis[129)]

(1) Meaning

The goal is to understand the opportunities and threats confronting the firm and to use this understanding to identify strategies that will enable the company to outperform its rivals.

(2) Opportunities

Opportunities arise when a company can take advantage of conditions in its environment to formulate and implement strategies that enable it to become more profitable.

(3) Threats

Threats arise when conditions in the external environment endanger the integrity and profitability of the company's business.

129 Charles W.L. Hill and Gareth R. Jones, Strategic Management Theory, Houghton Mifflink, 2003, pp.43-72.

(4) Porter's Five Forces Model

The main technique used to analyze competition in the industry environment is the five forces model. The five forces are

1) the risk of new entry by potential competitors,

2) the extent of rivalry among established firms,

3) the bargaining power of buyers,

4) the bargaining power of suppliers,

5) the threat of substitute products.

Porter's Five Forces Model[130)]

How the Five Forces Shape Competition within an Industry

The stronger that each of these five forces is, the more limited is the ability of established companies to raise prices and earn greater profits within their indus

1. A weak competitive force .....
   - may be viewed as an opportunity
   - as it allows company to earn greater profits
2. A strong competitive force .....
   - may be viewed as a threat
   - as it depresses industry profits
3. Strength of forces may change
   - as industry conditions change

Through its choice of actions, a company may alter the strength of one or more of the five forces to its advantage.

130 Source: Michael E. Porter, Competitive Strategy: Techniques for Analyzing Industries and Competitors, The Free Press, 1980, p. 4.

Identifying Key Success Factors ↓
How can we survive competition? ↓
<u>Analysis of competition</u> What drives competition? What are the main dimensions of competition? How intense is competition? How can we obtain a superior competitive position? ↓
Key Success Factors

C. Business Strategy[131)]

1. Meaning

Business-level strategy is concerned with how a firm competes within a particular business to establish competitive advantage over its rivals and four principal ones can be identified : cost leadership, focused cost leadership, differentiation and focused differentiation. For instance, Wal-mart inbound

131 Michael A. Hitt and R. Duane Ireland and Robert E. Hoskisson, Strategic Management, Thomas Southwestern, 2005, pp.149-186.

logistics and distribution system is faster, cheaper and efficient than rival. Wal-mart's operations are focused on cost-leadership and differentiation.

2. Abell's Business Definition process

To create a successful business model, managers must choose business-level strategies that give a company a competitive advantage over its rivals : that is, they must optimize competitive positioning. They must first decide on what it to be satisfied(Customer needs), Who is to be satisfied(Customer group), How Customer needs are to be satisfied(distinctive Competencies).

3. Cost Leadership strategy

(1) Meaning

A company's business model in pursuing a cost-leadership strategy is based on doing everything it can to lower its cost structure so it can make and sell goods or services at a lower cost than its competitors.

(2) Advantages

- Focused cost leadership is developing the right strategies to serve just one or two market segments.
- Targets the average customer.
- Protected from new entrants by cost advantage.

(3) Disadvantages

- Tied to maintaining low labor costs.
- Competitors may be able to imitate the cost-leader's methods.

4. Differentiation Strategy

(1) Meaning

A differentiation business model is based on creating a product that customers perceive as different or distinct in some important way.

(2) Advantages

- Focused differentiation is providing a differentiated product for just one or two market segments.
- Protected from industry competitors and new entrants by brand loyalty.

(3) Disadvantages

Competitors may be able to imitate a differentiator's product.

5. Market Development and Customer Groups[132)]

Companies must face the challenges of developing and maintaining a competitive strategy in : Fragmented industries, Embryonic Industries, Growth industries, Mature industries and declining industries. Company must be prepared to cross the chasm between the early adopters and the early majority.

132 Charles W.L. Hill and Gareth R. Jones, Strategic Management Theory, Houghton Mifflink, 2003, pp.358-361.

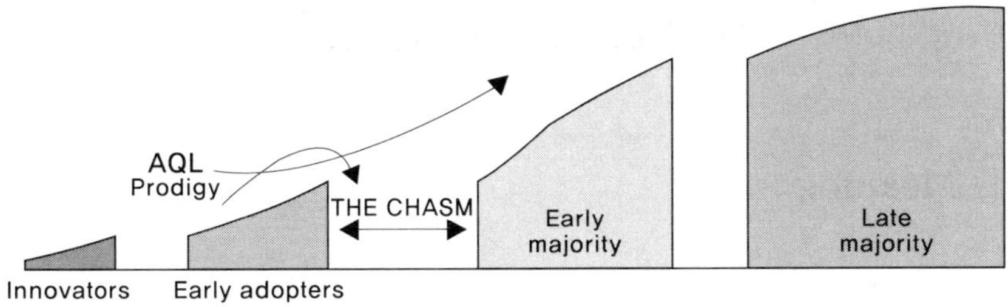

6. Failures in Competitive Positioning

Many companies, through neglect, ignorance, or error, do not work to continually improve their business model, do not perform strategic-group analysis, and often fail to identify and respond to changing opportunities and threats. As result, their business-level strategies do not work together, their business model starts to fail and their profitability starts to decline.

D. Corporate Strategy[133)]

1. Meaning

Corporate strategy defines the scope of a firm's businesses to maximize long-term profitability.

2. Type of Corporate Strategies

(1) Scope

1) Horizontal Integration

2) Vertical

3) Diversification

4) Strategic Outsourcing

133 Michael A. Hitt and R. Duane Ireland and Robert E. Hoskisson, Strategic Management, Thomas Southwestern, 2005, pp.304-372.

(2) Mode

1) Acquisition

2) Joint venture

3) Strategic alliance

4) M&A(Merger & Acquisition)

3. Horizontal Integration and Strategic Outsourcing etc

(1) Horizontal Integration

Horizontal integration can be understood as a way of trying to increase the profitability of company by reducing costs, increasing the value of the company's products through differentiation. But the company can bring into direct conflict with antitrust authorities by mergers and acquisitions.

(2) Vertical Integration

Vertical integration can enable a company to achieve a competitive advantage by helping build barriers to entry, facilitating investment in specialized assets, but vertical integration include increasing bureaucratic costs.

(3) Diversification

1) unrelated diversification

Companies pursuing a strategy of unrelated diversification have no intention of transferring or leveraging competencies between business units, their focus is on developing a multibusiness model that will strengthen the business model of each individual business unit.

2) Related diversification

By contrast, the multibusiness model in related diversification is based on transferring and leveraging competencies, sharing resources and building products. Lowers the cost of value creation activities in the diversified business.

Synergies from sharing resources across businesses(branch, joint R&D) and the ability to apply common management capabilities to different business.

(4) Strategic Outsourcing

The strategic Outsourcing of Noncore value creation activities may allow a company to lower its cost and better differentiate its products, But Outsourcing may have loss of information.

4. Strategic Alliances and M & As etc[134)]

(1) Acquisitions

Acquisitions are often favored as an entry strategy when the company lacks important competencies(resources and capabilities) required to compete in an area, but it can purchase an

134 Michael A. Hitt and R. Duane Ireland and Robert E. Hoskisson, Strategic Management, Thomas Southwestern, 2005, pp.475–478.

incumbent company that has those competencies and do so at a reasonable price.

Acquisitions also tend to be favored when the barriers to entry into the target industry are high and the company is unwilling to accept the time frame, development costs, and risks of internal new venturing.

(2) Joint venture

Joint ventures may be the preferred entry strategy when 1) the risks and costs associated with setting up a new business unit are more than the company is willing to assume on its own and 2) the company can increase the probability of successfully establishing a new business by teaming up with another company that has skills and assets complementing its own.

Joint ventures are not used as much as acquisitions and internal new ventures to establish business units in another industry. Rather, they are used to strengthen the business models of a company's existing divisions, such as when

SONY formed an alliance with SAMSUNG to work together to become dominant partners in the flat-screen LCD industry.

(3) Strategic Alliances

A Company can increase the probability of success by teaming up with another company with complementary skills. The advantages of alliances are that they facilitate entry into foreign markets, to share the fixed costs and risks etc.

(4) M & A(Merger & Acquisition)

M & A is attractive when company's competencies important in a new business area are lacking in the acquiring firm, to move quickly, value-chin activities and is protected by high barriers to entry. Pitfall of acquisition's company is that properly screen, overestimate, underestimating the expense and failing to follow through on post-merger/acquisition integration(PMI) of the acquired firm.

5. Reviewing the Corporate Portfolio

The BCG model is simplistic, Considers only two competitive environment factors, relative market share and industry growth rate.

▶ MEMO ◀

Chapter. VII
PROPERTY

A. Nature of Real Property

B. Estates in Real Property

C. Sale of Real Property

D. Landlord-Tenant

E. Mortgage

A. Nature of Real Property[135)]

1. Definition

Real Property is land or that is attached to the land in such a way that it is permanent, fixed, and immovable.

We need to define a few terms. A grantor is an owner who conveys his property, or some interest in it, to someone else. If you sell your house to "J" you are the grantor and she is the grantee.

2. Kind of Real Property

(1) Land

Land is the most common and important form of real property. In England, land was historically the greatest source of wealth and social status, far more important than industrial or commercial

135 Beth Walstom–Dunham, Introducation to LAW, Delmar Cengage Learning, 2009, pp.370–412.

enterprises.

As a result, the law of real property has been of paramount importance for nearly 1,000 years, developing very gradually to reflect changing conditions, Some real property terms sound medieval for the simple reason that they are medieval. By contrast, the common law of torts and contracts is comparatively new.

(2) Buildings

Building are real property. Houses, office buildings and factories all fall in this category.

(3) Subsurface Rights

In most states, the owner of the land also owns anything face rights may be worth far more than the surface land, for example if there is oil or gold underfoot. Although the land ownership generally owns these rights, she may sell them, while retaining ownership of the surface land.

Suppose Jun buys land in the country to get away from the materialistic rat race and then discovers natural gas under the surface. She may choose to sell the natural gas rights to an energy company. Jun keeps the rights to use the surface for whatever she wishes, and may later sell these rights to anyone she pleases, but the energy company owns the sub surface rights. It will have the right of enter Jun's land, drill for the gas, and conduct it away by pipe. The company could also sell the sub surface right, if it wished.

(4) Air Rights

The owner of land owns the air space above the land. Suppose you own an urban parking lot. The owner of an adjacent office building wishes to build a walkway across your parking lot to join her building with a neighboring skyscraper.

The office owner needs your permission to build across the air space and will expect to pay you a handsome fee for the privilege. Some companies, such as railroads, own a great deal of air space and earn considerable coin selling thin air.

(5) Plant Life

Plant life growing on land is real property, whether the plants are naturally occurring, such as trees, or cultivated crops. When a landowners sells his property, plant life is automatically included in the sale, unless the parties agree otherwise.

A landowner may also sell the plant life separately, if he wishes. A sale of the plant life alone, without the land, is a sale of goods.

(6) Fixtures

Fixtures are goods that have become attached to real property. A house contains many fixtures. The furnace and heating ducts were goods when they were manufactured and when they were sold to the builder, because they were movable. But when the builder attached them to the house, the items become fixtures.

By contrast, neither the refrigerator nor the grand piano is a fixture. When an owner sells real property, the buyer normally obtains the fixtures, unless the parties specify otherwise. Sometimes it is difficult to determine whether something is a fixture.

B. Estates in Real Property

1. Fee Simple Absolute

The owner of a freehold estate has the present right to possess the property and to use it in any lawful way she wants.

A fee simple absolute provides the owner with the greatest possible control of the property. When we think of buying a house or owning land outright, we are usually referring to fee simple absolute, the most common form of land ownership. Suppose Jun inherits a fee simple interest in a 10 acre(acre:4,046.8m^2) vineyard. Jun may use the land for any purpose that the law allows. She may continue to raise grapes, or, if she hates wine, she may rip up the vines and plant apple trees, build a condominium complex, or allow the land to go to waste. Although zoning laws may regulate her use, nothing in Jun's estate itself limits her use of the land.

2. Non Freehold Estates

A non freehold is entirely different from the freehold estates. It involves a lease in which the owner, the landlord, agrees to permit a tenant to use and possess the property. When you lease an apartment from a landlord, you have a leasehold or a non-freehold estate.

3. Concurrent Estates[136)]

When two or more people own real property at the same time, they have concurrent estates.

136 John M. Scheb Ⅱ and Hemant Sharma, An Introduction to the Amercian Legal System, Wolters Kluwer-Law&Business, 2012, pp.214-218.

The most common form of concurrent estates are tenancy in common, joint tenancy, marital property, and condominiums and cooperatives.

(1) Tenancy in Common

The most common form of concurrent estate is tenancy in common. Suppose Kim owns a house or, in legal terms, owns a fee simple absolute estate in the house. Kim agrees to sell her house to park and lee. When she conveys the deed, that is, transfers the deed, to "part and lee", those two now have a tenancy in common. This kind of estate can also be created in a will. If Kim had died still owing the house, and left it in her will to "park and lee" then "park and lee" would have a tenancy in common.

A tenancy in common might have 2 owners. Each owner is called a tenant in common or co-tenant. They own an equal interest in the entire property. Any co-tenant may convey her interest in the property to another person. Further, when a co-tenant dies, her interest in the property passes to her heirs.

(2) Marital Property

Two forms of concurrent ownership are available only to married couples : tenancy by the entirety and community property.

1) Tenancy by the Entirety

This form of ownership exists in slightly over half of the states. The husband and wife each own the entire property, and they both have a right of survivorship.

So when the husband died, his one-half interest in the property automatically passes to his wife. If the parties wish to sell their interests, they must do so together.

2) Community Property

This system allows the husband and wife to maintain separate ownership of assets they bring to the marriage or inherit. Those assets are called separate property. They remain the private property of each spouse during the marriage.

Either spouse may convey separate property to another person during the marriage and may leave the separate property to anyone he or she wishes. But income or assets that either party earns during the marriage are considered community property, which must be equally shared during the marriage, regardless of who earns it. Neither party may convey community property without the concent of the other. When a spouse dies, one-half of the community property goes to the surviving spouse, and the other half goes to the heirs of the deceased.

C. Sale of Real Property[137)]

For most people, buying or selling a house is the biggest, most important financial transaction They will make.

137 Beth Walstom-Dunham, Introducation to LAW, Delmar Cengage Learning, 2009, pp.384-388.

1. Seller's obligation Concerning the property

Historically, the common law recognized the rule of caveat emptier in the sale of real property that is, let the buyer beware.

If a buyer walked into his new living room and fell through the floor into a lake of toxic waste, it was his tough luck. But the common law changes with the times, and today courts place an increasing burden of fairness on the sellers of real estate. Two of the most significant obligation are the implied warranty of habitability and the duty to disclose defects.

(1) Implied warranty of Habitability

Most states now impose an implied warranty of habitability on a builder who sells a new home. This means that, whether he wants to or not, the builder is guaranteeing that the new house contains adequate materials and good workmanship.

In many states, the warranty extends for

reasonable time, not only the original purchaser but to subsequent buyers as well.

(2) Duty of Disclose Defects

The seller of a home must disclose facts that a buyer does not know and can not readily observe, if they materially affect the property's value.

2. Sale Contract and title Examination

The statute of frauds requires that an agreement to sell real property must be in writing to be enforceable. A contract for the sale of a house is often several pages of dense legal reading, in which the lawyers for the buyer and seller attempt to allocate risks for every problem that might go wrong. A written contract for the sale of land is generally valid if it includes the names of all parties, a precise description of the property being sold, the price and signatures.

3. Closing and Deeds

While the buy is checking the seller's title, she also probable needs to arrange financing, as describe below in the section on mortgages. When the title work is complete and the buyer has arranged financing, the parties arrange a closing, a meeting at which the property is actually sold.

The seller signs the deed over to the buyer in exchange for the purchase price. The buyer pays the price either with a certified check(保證手票) or by having her lender pay. If a lender pays part or all of the price, the buyer executes a mortgage to the lender as part of the closing.

4. Recording

Recording the deed means it with the official state registry. The registry clerk places a photocopy of the deed in the agency's bound volumes and indexes the deed by the name of the grantor and the grantee. Recording is a critical step in the sale of land, because it puts all the world on notice that the grantor has sold the land. It has tittle effect between grantor and grantee.

Suppose kim sells his farm to lee for $100,000. Lee records her deed within minutes of the purchase. The public is now on notice that Lee owns the property. A month later Kim offers to sell the land to Park for $80,000. Park must check the registry, where she will quickly learn that Kim does not own the land. Suppose that, without checking the registry deeds, Park pays the full amount and Kim gives her a fraudulent deed. Lee's property is safe, and Park gets nothing. She was obligated to search the registry before buying. Park has a valid claim against Kim, but if he has skipped town, the claim may be useless.

By contrast, suppose that Kim sells the land to Lee, who fails to record his deed, A week later, Kim offers the same property to Park, who checks the registry and sees no mention of the sale to Lee. If Park pays for the land, he will probable get valid title to it because he is a bona fide purchaser, that is, someone who gives value or money in good faith for property. Park believed in good faith that Kim owned the farm, since his search of the registry indicated no defects in his title. A bona fide purchaser generally takes the land over a buyer(Lee) who failed to record.

D. Landlord–Tenant[138)]

1. Definition

When an owner of a freehold estate allows an other person temporary, exclusive possession of the property, the parties have created a landlord–tenant relationship. The statute of frauds generally requires that a lease be in writing. Some states will enforce an oral lease if it is for a short

138 Jeffrey F. Beatty and Susan S. Samuelson, Business Law and the Legal Environment, Thomson Southwestern, 2004, pp.1062–1077; John M. Scheb Ⅱ and Hemant Sharma, An Introduction to the American Legal System, Wolters Kluwer–Law&Business, 2012, pp.219–221.

term, such as one year or less, but even when an oral lease is permitted, it is wiser for the parties to put their agreement in writing, because a written lease avoids many misunderstandings.

2. Landlord's Duties[139)]

(1) Duty Deliver Possession

The landlord's first important duty is to deliver possession of the premisses at the beginning of the tenancy, that is, to make the rented space available to the tenant. In most cases this presents no problems and the new tenant moves in. But what happens if the previous tenant has refused to leave when the new tenancy begins.

The English rule obligates the landlord to remove the previous tenant in time rule. If the old tenant is still in possession when the new tenant arrives, the landlord has breached the lease.

139 Robert J. Aaiberts, Real Estate Law, Gengage Learning, 2015, pp.426-466.

(2) Quiet Enjoyment

All tenants are entitled to quiet enjoyment of the premises, meaning the right to use the property without the interference of the landlord.

The most common interference with quiet enjoyment is an eviction, meaning some act that forces the tenant to abandon the premises. Of course, some evictions are legal, as when a tenant fails to pay the rent. But some evictions are illegal. There are two types of eviction : actual and constructive.

1) Actual Eviction

If a landlord prevents the tenant from possessing the premises, he has actually evicted her. Suppose a landlord decides that a group of students are "trouble makers". Without going through lawful eviction procedures in court, the landlord simply waits until the students are out of the apartment and changes all the locks.

By denying the students access to premises, the landlord has actually evicted them and has breached their right of quiet enjoyment.

2) Constructive Eviction

If a landlord substantially interferes with the tenant's use and enjoyment of the premise, he has constructively evicted her. To claim a constructive eviction, the tenant must vacate the premises.

The tenant must also prove that the interference was sufficiently serious and lasted long enough that she was forced to move out. A lack of hot water for two days is not fatal, but lack of any water for two weeks creates a constructive eviction.

(3) Duty to Maintain Premises

In most states, a landlord has a duty to deliver the premises in a habitable condition and a continuing duty to maintain the habitable condition. This duty overlaps with the quiet enjoyment obligation, but it is not identical.

1) Lease

The lease itself generally obligates the landlord to maintain the exterior of any building and the common areas. If a lease does not do so, state law may imply the obligation

2) Implied Warranty of Habitability

The implied warranty of habitability requires that a landlord meet all standards set by the local building code, or that premises be fit human habitation.

Suppose, The landlord breached the implied warranty. The tenant had complained repeatedly about a variety of problems. The washer and dryer, which were included in the lease, frequently failed. If the defect conditions seriously interfere with the tenancy, the court declares the implied warranty breached and orders a rent abatement, that is, a reduction in the rent owed. The long the defects continued and the greater their severity, the more the rent is abated.

3) Tenant Remedies for Defective Conditions

Many states allow a tenant to withhold rent, representing the decreased value of the premises.

■ Rent Withholding

The tenant must first notify the landlord of the problems and allow her reasonable period to make repairs. If she fails to remedy the problem, the tenant may then withhold a portion of the rent, while continuing to live in the premises. The tenant should withhold a portion of the rent that approximates the seriousness of the defective conditions.

■ Repair and Deduct

In some states, if a tenant notifies the landlord of a serious defect and the landlord fails to remedy the problem, the tenant may deduct a reasonable amount of money from the rental payment and have the repair made himself.

(4) Duty to Return Security Deposit

Most landlords requires tenants to pay a security deposit, in case the tenant damages the premises. In many states, a landlord must either return the security deposit soon after the tenant has moved out or notify the tenant of the damage and the cost of the repairs.

3. Tenant's Duties

(1) Duty to Pay Rent

The landlord's first important duty is to deliver possession of the premises at the tenant. If no rent is stated in the lease, either the leasehold will be considered a gift from the landlord or the tenant will be liable for the reasonable value of her possession of the property.[140)]

(2) Duty to Use premises for Proper Purpose

A lease normally lists what a tenant may do in the premises and prohibits other activities. For example, a residential lease allows the tenant to use the property for normal living purposes,

---

140 Robert J. Aaiberts, Real Estate Law, Gengage Learning, 2015, p.438.

but not for any retail, commercial, or industrial purpose. A landlord may evict a tenant who violates the lease by using the premises for prohibited purposes.

(3) Duty Not to Damage Premise

A tenant is liable to the landlord for any significant damage he causes to the property. The tenant is not liable for normal wear and tear. If, however, he knocks a hole in a wall or damages the plumbing, the landlord may collect the cost of repairs, either by using the security deposit or by suing, if necessary. A landlord may also seek to evict a tenant for serious damage to the property.

(4) Duty Not to Disturb Other Tenants

Most leases, commercial and residential, include a covenant that the tenant will not disturb other tenants in the building.

1) The test is reasonableness

A landlord may evict a tenant who unreasonably

disturbs others. The test is reasonableness. A landlord does not have the right to evict a residental tenant for giving one loud party but may evict a tenant who repeatedly plays loud music late at night and disturbs the quiet enjoyment of other tenants.

2) Animal Attacks

In most states, the owner of an animal is responsible for any harm it causes. A tenant is liable if her dog intimidates or attacks other tenants. The landlord may have the right to evict a tenant whose animal abuses other tenant or landlord.

4. Change in the Parties

Sometimes the parties to a lease change. This can happen when the landlord sells the property or when a tenant wants to turn the leased property over to another tenant.

(1) Sale of the Property

Generally, the sale of leased property does not affect the lease but merely substitutes one landlord, the purchaser, for another, the seller. The remains valid, and the tenant enjoys all rights and obligations until the end of the term. The new landlord may not raise the rent during the period of the existing lease or make any other changes in the tenant's rights.

There is one exception. If the tenant is not in possession when the property is sold and the tenant's lease was never recorded with the registry of deeds, then the buyer need not honor the lease. If the buyer has no way of knowing there is a tenant, she should not be required to respect the lease.

(2) Assignment and Sublease

1) Assignment

A tenant who wishes to turn the property over to another tenant will attempt to assign the lease or to sublet it. In an assignment, the tenant transfer all of his legal interest to the other party. The orignal tenant is the assignor and the new tenant is the assignee.

If a tenant validly assigns a lease, the assignee obtains all rights and liabilities under the lease. This means that if the new tenant fails to pay the rent on time, the landlord can sue both parties, old and new, seeking to evict both and to recover the unpaid rent from both. A landlord generally insists on a covenant in the lease prohibiting the tenant from assigning without the landlord's written permission.

2) Sublease

In a sublease, the tenant remains a tenant of the landlord and turns over some of his rights to a new tenant. The original tenant is the sublessor and the new tenant is the sublessee. The sublessor remains fully liable to the landlord for all provisions of the lease, including payment of rent and proper care of the premises. The sublessee has no legal relationship with the landlord, but has a normal tenant's obligations to the sublessor.

The sublessee must pay rent to the sublessor and must return the property in good condition at the end of the sublease. Must a landlord agree to a sublease? The rules are essentially the same as for and assignment. The lease probably requires the tenant to obtain the landlord's permission before subletting.

(3) Injuries

You invite a friend to dinner in your rented home, but after the meal she slips and falls, seriously injuring her back. Are you liable? Is the landlord?

1) Tenant's Liability

A tenant is generally liable for injuries occurring within the premises she is leasing, whether that is an apartment, a store, or otherwise. If a tenant permits grease to accumulate on a kitchen floor and a guest slips and fails, the tenant is liable.

Generally, a tenant is not liable for injuries occurring in common areas over which she has no control, such as exterior walkways. If a tenant's dinner guest falls because the building's common stairway has loose steps, the landlord is probably liable.

2) Landlord's Liability[141)]

At common law, a landlord had very limited liability for injuries on the premises, but today many courts requires a landlord to use reasonable care and hold her liable for foreseeable harm.

Landlord may be liable in negligence to tenants or their guests for criminal attacks on the premises. Court determine liability by looking at factors such as the nature of the crime, what a reasonable landlord would have done to prevent it, and the foreseeable of the attack.

141 Robert J. Aaiberts, Real Estate Law, Gengage Learning, 2015, pp.460–463.

E. Mortgage[142)]

1. Definition[143)]

A mortgage is an interest in land created by a written instrument providing security for the performance of a duty or the payment of a debt. If the mortgagor does not pay the mortgage debt on time, the mortgagee(or the party to whom the debt is owned) has two choices. It can either assume title to the piece of real property or call property to be sold and keep the proceeds toward satisfaction of the mortgage debt.

142 John M. Scheb Ⅱ and Hemant Sharma, An Introduction to the Amercian Legal System, Wolters Kluwer-Law&Business, 2012, pp.212-214.

143 Jeffrey F. Beatty and Susan S. Samuelson, Business Law and the Legal Environment, Thomson Southwestern, 2004, p.1050; A mortgage is a security interest in real property. The homeowner who borrows money is the mortgagor, because she is giving the mortgage to the lender. The lender, In turn, is the mortgagee, the party acquiring a security interest.

2. Parties Involved in Transaction

The mortgagor creates the mortgage. He is the "landowner" and debtor. The mortgagee is the creditor(eg. bank) and the holder of the mortgage.

3. Types of Mortgage Theories [144)]

(1) Lien Theory Jurisdiction

In the majority of states, the mortgage creates only a lien on the land regardless of the operative words of the mortgage instrument. Under lien theory, the mortgagor remains the owner of the land and the mortgagee holds only a security interest in the land.

Therefore, the mortgagor retains possession unless a foreclosure takes place, in which case the mortgagee may take over possession of the land.

---

144 John M. Scheb II and Hemant Sharma, An Introduction to the Amercian Legal System, Wolters Kluwer–Law&Business, 2012, p.212.

(2) Title Theory Jurisdiction

At common law, and still in about 20 states, the mortgage operates as a conveyance of the legal title to the mortgagee. Note, however, that such title is subject to defeasance on payment of the mortgage debt.

However, under a title theory, the mortgagee is actually entitled to possession of the land at any time. Practically, this means that the mortgagee may take possession immediately upon default and need not wait for foreclosure.

4. Conveyance of Encumbered Property

Where a mortgage exists on property at the time that the mortgagor conveys the property to a third party, the language in the deed controls whether the third party assumes liability for the mortgage debt. At Common law, the mortgagee could not object to the mortgagor's transfer of the property.

(1) Subject to Mortgage

In a conveyance of land where the deed states that the buyer or grantee takes "subject to" a mortgage, the grantee is not personally liable for the mortgage debt.

However, if she does not pay the debt, the mortgage may be foreclosed and she(the grantee) will lose the land.

(2) Assumption of mortgage

In a sale of land in which the deed states that the purchaser "assumes" the mortgage, the purchaser or grantee is personally liable for the mortgage debt and is subject to deficiency judgment in the event that a foreclosure sale does not satisfy the debt. Where the grantee assumes the mortgage but does not pay, she is primarily liable to the mortgage, but the original mortgagor remains secondarily liable and may be called to pay if the mortgagee does not exceed as against the grantee.

Note also that the mortgagee and grantee can

contract so that the original mortgagor retains no liability.

(3) Deed Language is silent

Where the deed language is silent, the grantee is considered to take "subject to" the mortgage.

(4) Recording

The mortgage(as well as any assignments thereof)should be recorded. Failure to recorded the mortgage may make it possible for the mortgagor to convey to a bona fide purchaser who would take free of the mortgage under the recording act.

5. Foreclosure

(1) Modern Day Application

In most jurisdictions today, foreclosure is the method by which the security, or proceeds from the sale thereof, is applied to the satisfaction of the debt or obligation.

It is also the means by which the mortgagee succeeds in ending the mortgagor's ownership interest in the real estate. Before a foreclosure may take place, the mortgagor's ownership interest in the real estate. Before a foreclosure may take place, the mortgagor must default on the loan.[145)]

(2) Right of Redemption

The right of redemption allows a mortgagor in default to pay off the amount owed to the mortgagee and any interest prior to foreclosure.

If the mortgagor actually pays off the debt prior to the foreclosure, he redeems the mortgage and takes the land free of the mortgage even though he had previously defaulted.

---

145 Jeffrey F. Beatty and Susan S. Samuelson, Business Law and the Legal Environment, Thomson Southwestern, 2004, p.1050; The mortgagee in most cases obtains a lien on the house, meaning the right to foreclose on the property if the mortgagor fails to pay back the money borrowed. A mortgagee forecloses by taking legal possession of the property, auctioning it to the highest bidder, and using the proceeds to pay off the loan.

1) Equitable Redemption

Under Equitable redemption, the mortgagor must redeem before the foreclosure sale. Once the foreclosure sale has occurred, the mortgagor's rights to redeem are terminated.

2) Statutory Redemption

Under a statutory redemption theory, a mortgagor may redeem even after the foreclosure sale has occurred. This period is usually six months to a year. About fifty percent of the states grant the mortgagor a right of statutory redemption.

(3) Other Methods of Foreclosure

In some states, other methods of foreclosure are available. Foreclosure by sale under judicial supervision facilitates the determination of the value of the mortgaged property and thus aids in the determination of the amount of any deficiency decree that might be awarded where the proceeds realized from the sale are insufficient to satisfy the mortgage debt.

(4) Case Analysis

1) Question :

A owned a 500–acre(1acre=4,046m^2) ranch that was used for raising horses, cattle and sheep. The property known as high wall was located in west Texas. In 2010 A sold high wall to B for the purchase price of $ 1,000,000. According to the terms of their land sale agreement, B paid A a down payment of $ 250,000 and A agreed to carry a mortgage for the balance. The parties then executed a mortgage as security for a $ 750,000 promissory note that was due in 2020 with a 7% interest per annum. The mortgage, which named A as mortgagee, was properly recorded.

In 2013 B defaulted on his mortgage payment and A instituted a foreclosure action on the property. At the foreclosure sale A, who was one of the bidders, bought back high wall for $ 500,000. At the time of the foreclosure sale, high wall had a fair market value of $ 1,500,000.

Two weeks later, B win the seoul lottery and collected $ 1,700,000. He mow seeks to pay off the $ 750,000 mortgage debt and re–acquire the property. However, A has refused to honor any redemption.

B has filed suit against A seeking an order allowing him to pay off the mortgage(with accumulated interest) and set aside the foreclosure sale. If the court rules in favor of B, it will likely be due to the fact that

(a) B has an equitable right of redemption.

(b) B has a statutory right of redemption.

(c) A purchase at the foreclosure sale clogged B's right of redemption.

(d) A did not pay fair market value at the foreclosure sale.

2) Answer :

(a) It is wrong because after the foreclosure sale technically there is no equitable right to redemption.

(b) Statutes providing for redemption from foreclosure sale universally permit mortgagors or their successors in interest to exercise the right.

(c) It is incorrect because the term "clogging" is usually used to prevent the mortgagee from inserting terms in the mortgage instrument limiting or restricting the mortgagor's not mortgagee's right of redemption(e.g, a provision limiting redemption to the mortgagor himself).

(d) It is wrong because it is difficult for a mortgagor to upset a(foreclosure) sale. According to Burke, a mortgagor must show fraud or a gross irregularity in the conduct of the sale; the inadequacy of the sale price, standing alone, is not a basic for avoiding it. Inadequacy coupled with frand, however, will upset the sale. Real Estate transaction.

6. Deficiency Judgments

A deficiency judgment only comes into play when the mortgagor has defaulted in the mortgage debt and the mortgagee has sold the real property at a foreclosure sale.

If at the foreclosure sale, the mortgagee receives enough money for the property to pay off the mortgage debt, the mortgagor has no further obligation. However, where the proceeds from the foreclosure sale do not completely cover the mortgage debt, a deficiency is said to exist.

In most states, a mortgagee may proceed directly against the mortgagor for the balance of the loan. This money needed to satisfy the mortgage loan is called a deficiency judgment.

▶ MEMO ◀

Reference

Austin Sarat and Patricial Ewick, The Handbook of Law and Society, Willey Blackwell, 2015.

Beth Walstom–Dunham, Introduction to Law, Delmar cengage Learning, 2009.

Bethel v. New York City Transit Authority, Cout of Appeals of New York, 1998.

Bradford Stone, Unifrom Commercial Code in a Nutshell, Thomson West, 2002.

Charles H. Whitebread and Christopher Slobogin, Criminal Procedure–an analysis of cases and concepts, Thomson West, 2003.

Charles W.L. Hill and Gareth R. Jones, Strategic Management Theory, Houghton Mifflink, 2003.

Claud D. Rhhwer and Anthony M. Skrocki, Contracts, West Group, 2002.

E.allan Farnsworth and William F. Young, Selections for Contracts, Thomson west, Foundation Press, New york, 2003.

Jaap Hage and Bram Akkermans, Introduction to Law, Springer International Publishing Switzerlan, 2014.

Jeffrey F. Beatty and Susan S. Samuelson, Business Law and the Legal Environment, Thomson Southwestern, 2004.

John F. Dolan, Commercial Law–Essential Terms and Transactins, Aspen Law Business, 1997.

John M. Scheb Ⅱ and Hemant Sharma, An Introduction to the Amercian Legal System, Wolters Kluwer–Law&Business, 2012.
J.Scott Slorach and Jason Ellis, Business Law,–2015?2016–, Oxford University Press, 2014.

Marc A. Franklin and Robert L. Rabin, Tort Law and Alternatives –cases and materials–, Foundation Press, New York, 2001.

Matthew Lippman, Law and Society, SAGE Publications. Inc, 2015.

Michael A. Hitt and R. Duane Ireland and Robert E. Hoskisson, Strategic Management, Thomas Southwestern, 2005.

Multistate Legal Students, INC, PMBR part a–multistate specialist–, Multistate Legal Students, INC, 2004.

Richard E. Speidel and Lan Ayres, Contract Law, Foundation Press, New York, 2003.

Robert J. Aaiberts, Real Estate Law, Gengage Learning, 2015.

Terry Halbert and Elaine ingulli, and Law & Ethics in the Business Environment, Cengage Learning, 2015.

Trimarco v. Klein, Court of Appeals of New York, 1982.

William A. Klein and J.Mark Ramseyer and Stephen M. Bainbridge, Foundation Press, 2003.

저자 약력

全將憲(전장헌)

- 단국대학교 일반대학원 법학박사 과정수료
  법학박사(민사법 전공)
- Northwestern University School of Law Master of Laws
- 한국금융연수원 민법 및 민사집행법
  (노동부지원 자문교수)
- 한국고시정보 민법전문위원
- 경기대학교 법무사시험 민사집행법 강사
- KBS-2TV, 각 신문사 민사집행법 특강 및 논단
- 성균관대학교 행정대학원 민사집행법 강사
- 연세대학교 경영대학원 상남경영원 법학강사
- 한국산업인력관리공단 감정평가사 민법강사
- 소방공무원시험 면접위원 등
- 건국대학교 법과대학 법학과 강사
- 국민건강보험관리공단 소송실무 강사
- 법무부 법 교육 강사
- 태학관 법정연구회 민법 강사
- 건대·중앙대·덕성여대·연세대·한양대 법학 강사
- 파주시·안양시·용인시 민법 강사
- 사단법인 한국지적재산권 법제연구원 책임연구원
- 재) 건설산업교육원 초빙교수
- Visiting Scholar University of Washington
- 경민대학교 민법 겸임교수
- 한세대학교 민법 전임강사
- 한국대학협의회 출제위원 등
- 중앙대학교 법과대학 법학강사
- 한국부동산법학회 부회장
- 한국법학회 부회장
- 단국대학교 특수대학원 특수법무학과 주임교수
- 단국대학교 법정대학 법무행정학과 교수/학과장

主要 著書 및 論文

- 「민법강의」
- 「민법연습」
- 「민법총칙」
- 「객관식 민법 및 민사특별법」
- 「민법이론」
- 「법학원론」
- 「민법과 민사집행법의 관계」
- 「민사소송에서 민사집행까지」
- 「부동산 경매의 투자와 함정」
- 「부동산경매 제1권, 제3권」
- 「부동산 사법」
- 「선의취득의 요건에 관한 연구」
- 「민법의 상린관계와 건축법의 접점에 관한 연구」
- 「불법행위에 따른 손해배상의 범위」
- 「저당권 실행에 관한 연구」

merican Law

판 1쇄 발행 / 2016년 8월 29일
판 3쇄 발행 / 2018년 8월 24일

자 전장헌
행처 형설출판사
경기도 파주시 회동길 37-23 · 전화 (031) 955-2361～4 · 팩시밀리 (031) 955-2341
행인 장진혁
록 라－제9호 · 1962년 5월 1일
페이지 http://www.hyungseul.co.kr
mail hs@hyungseul.co.kr

가 16,000원

3N 978-89-472-8106-5 93360

이 도서의 국립중앙도서관 출판시도서목록(CIP)은 서지정보유통지원시스템 홈페이지(http://seoji.nl.go.kr)와 국가자료공동목록시스템(http://www.nl.go.kr/kolisnet)에서 이용하실 수 있습니다.(CIP제어번호 : CIP2016017850)

AMERICAN LAW